CULTURE SMART!

AUSTRALIA

Barry Penney and Gina Teague

·K·U·P·E·R·A·R·D·

ISBN 978 1 85733 828 7

British Library Cataloguing in Publication Data
A CIP catalogue entry for this book is available from the
British Library

First published in Great Britain
by Kuperard, an imprint of Bravo Ltd
59 Hutton Grove, London N12 8DS
Tel: +44 (0) 20 8446 2440   Fax: +44 (0) 20 8446 2441
www.culturesmart.co.uk
Inquiries: sales@kuperard.co.uk

Series Editor Geoffrey Chesler
Design Bobby Birchall

Printed in India

About the Author

BARRY PENNEY is an Australian teacher, trainer, and management executive. After graduating from the University of Adelaide, he worked in education before specializing in sales, sales management, and marketing for several multinational corporations. He went on to study at The Australian Administrative Staff College, Victoria. Barry has lived and worked in the United States, Britain, and Turkey. On returning to Australia he established a management training business and devised and conducted marketing and presentation courses. He has published several short stories, and teaches English to foreign language students. He is an Associate Fellow of the Australian Institute of Management.

GINA TEAGUE is a consultant, trainer, and writer on cross-cultural management, international relocation, and global career development. She has lived and worked in France, Spain, Brazil, the USA, and Australia. During her sixteen years in New York, Gina gained an M.A. in Organizational Psychology and an Ed.M. in Counseling Psychology from Columbia University. Since moving to Australia, in 2003, she has become a licensed organizational psychologist, developed a successful intercultural consultancy, and is an Asia–Pacific based trainer for the United Nations.

The Culture Smart! series is continuing to expand. All Culture Smart! guides are available as e-books, and many as audio books. For latest titles visit

www.culturesmart.co.uk

The publishers would like to thank **CultureSmart!**Consulting for its help in researching and developing the concept for this series.

CultureSmart!Consulting creates tailor-made seminars and consultancy programs to meet a wide range of corporate, public-sector, and individual needs. Whether delivering courses on multicultural team building in the USA, preparing Chinese engineers for a posting in Europe, training call-center staff in India, or raising the awareness of police forces to the needs of diverse ethnic communities, it provides essential, practical, and powerful skills worldwide to an increasingly international workforce.

For details, visit www.culturesmartconsulting.com

CultureSmart!Consulting and **CultureSmart!** guides have both contributed to and featured regularly in the weekly travel program "Fast Track" on BBC World TV..

contents

contents

Map of Australia

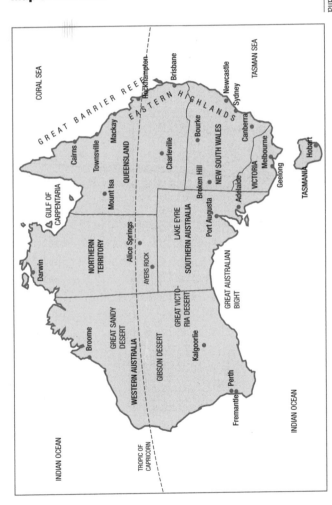

introduction

What makes Australia different? First, if you're traveling from Southeast Asia, you'll cover about 4,500 miles (7,240 km); if from the Americas or South Africa, about 9,000 miles (14,500 km); if from Europe, about 10,500 miles (17,000 km). It's not just a quick crossing by ferryboat, or a walk over a bridge. It's a long way to "Down Under." So there are bound to be cultural as well as geographical differences.

And then there's the size of it. It's a long way from one side to the other. Perth, the capital of Western Australia, is the most isolated city in the world. It is closer to Singapore than to Sydney, which is about 1,900 miles (3,000 km) away.

Most countries have probably had a fairly steady population growth, with much the same ethnic mix, for hundreds of years. Apart, of course, from the Aborigines, who have been there for over fifty thousand years, Australians have not been there long. The first Europeans settled just over two hundred years ago; Australia only widened/opened its doors to more diverse immigrant communities in the 1950s. Australia's population has doubled since 1957, transforming what was perhaps one of the dullest nations to one of the most stimulating, with many interesting differences of culture and custom.

Australians are generally warmhearted and generous. Perhaps they have taken the best from the immigrant cultures, blending them with the best of Aboriginal and early settler cultures—and, of course, also keeping a little of what was not the best. But Australians are mostly open, honest, and forthright, and will expect you to be the same. Early life in Australia was difficult; the result is an ethic of hard work and hard play. Australians work to live.

Today, Australia has one of the world's highest standards of living, fine food and wine, a great sporting tradition, a colorful and invigorating multiculturalism, and an affection for visitors.

This book sets out to provide more than just the nuts and bolts of where to stay, what to see, and how to travel. *Culture Smart!* guides are written for true travelers who want to understand the beliefs and attitudes of the people they meet: to learn from them, and to absorb the human dimension of the country. *Culture Smart! Australia* provides the necessary background information to enable you to put a human face on the country and its people; to communicate; to make friends; to share experiences; to enjoy the culture; and to form lasting relationships.

Key Facts

Official Name	Commonwealth of Australia	Member of the British Commonwealth
Capital City	Canberra	
Main Cities	Sydney, Melbourne, Brisbane, Adelaide, Perth, Hobart, Darwin.	
Area	2,966,136 sq. miles (7,682,300 sq. km)	
Climate	Ranges from tropical to temperate. Most of Australia is arid land or desert. The extreme north is tropical; the southeast and southwest more Mediterranean. The east coast and the Eastern Highlands are the areas of greatest rainfall.	
Population	23,734,616 (5 Feb 2015)	
Ethnic Makeup	Nationals from over 140 countries. Predominantly European descent. At the 2011 census, 53.7 percent of people had both parents born in Australia. 34.3 percent of people had both parents born overseas. 28 percent were born overseas.	
Family Makeup	Average family size 2.7; Average number of children 1.74.	
Language	English	Aboriginal and other languages are spoken at home and are available in government offices, banks, insurance houses, etc.
Religion	61.1 percent of Australians classify themselves Christian of which 25.3 percent identify as Catholic (2011 Census). Other religions include Eastern Orthodox, Jews, Muslims, and Hindus.	

Government	Democratic Federal system comprising six states and two territories. The states are New South Wales, Queensland, South Australia, Victoria, Western Australia, and Tasmania. The territories are the Northern Territory and the Australian Capital Territory.	
Seat of Federal Government	Canberra	
Media	Public broadcasters, ABC and SBS three major commercial television networks, and cable TV. Digital radio introduced in 2009. 75 percent of radio market dominated by commercial broadcasters include the ARN, Southern Cross Media, Nova, MRN, Fairfax Media, Grant Broadcasters. The public broadcaster ABC radio plus 288 community radio stations account for the remaining 25 percent. Two national and ten state/territory daily newspapers, thirty-seven regional dailies and 470 other regional and suburban newspapers.	
Electricity	230 volts, 50 Hz	Three-pronged plugs used. Adaptors are needed for most overseas appliances
Video/TV	Pal B system	Some systems will play NTSC TV.
Internet Domain	.au	
Telephone	Australia's country code is 61.	International and state codes are listed at the back of the telephone directory.
Currency	Australian dollar	
Time Difference	Australia has three time zones. Some areas have Daylight Saving.	Western: GMT+8 hrs Central: GMT+9.5 hrs Eastern: GMT+10 hrs For Daylight Saving add one hour.

LAND & PEOPLE

Australia is the world's largest island and its smallest continent. This is a country the size of the United States of America, spanning three time zones, yet with barely twenty-three million inhabitants. It is an ancient land, geologically one of the oldest on earth, and was first populated by the Aborigines and Torres Strait Islanders.

These original inhabitants are thought to have come south from Asia some fifty to seventy thousand years ago, when Australia was linked to Indonesia by a land bridge. In 1788 a handful

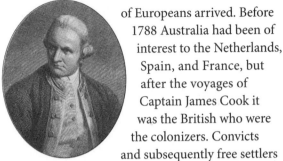

of Europeans arrived. Before 1788 Australia had been of interest to the Netherlands, Spain, and France, but after the voyages of Captain James Cook it was the British who were the colonizers. Convicts and subsequently free settlers from Britain and Ireland arrived to establish a thriving Anglo-Celtic society.

The early Europeans brought with them epidemics of smallpox, measles, and venereal diseases, and they also, occasionally, murdered Aborigines. At the time of white settlement the estimated black population was 700,000. By 1900, this figure had shrunk to 100,000. Much has been done in recent times, and much still needs to be done, to repair the damage.

Throughout the 1800s freed convicts, explorers, and settlers spread across the continent. Wheat growing, sheep and cattle ranching, the discovery of gold, and expanding immigration all contributed to spectacular economic growth.

From 1945, after the end of the Second World War, the immigration of many of Europe's dispossessed began what was to be one of the world's greatest exercises in multiculturalism.

Convict Ancestry

Most of those Australians who can claim convict ancestry have become quite proud of it. The fact is that, although described as "felons," these convicts had committed no serious crimes by today's definition of the word. Their offenses would be better described as "misdemeanors." In those days, stealing a sheep to feed one's family was a hanging offense. Those who were sent on the long, terrible voyage to Australia were recorded to have committed such offenses as stealing a round of cheese, a loaf of bread, or some lace handkerchiefs, or even opening a letter addressed to someone else.

This has been added to in recent years by an influx of immigrants from India, China, Vietnam, and the Philippines—plus a continued stream from the UK, New Zealand, and South Africa.

Today, one quarter of Australia's population was born overseas.

In 1988 the nation of Australia celebrated its Bicentennial—the two hundredth anniversary of the arrival of the first convict ships. As with the United States and Canada, also first colonized by the British, the Europeans displaced a native population that had been there for thousands of years. And, like the United States and Canada, Australia has become a powerful, industrialized nation with a high standard of living.

Settled and populated by Europeans for the first one hundred and fifty years, Australia was traditionally tied to Europe—and in particular to the mother country, Great Britain. In the last forty years or so, nearby Asian nations have become increasingly important.

Australia has undergone a significant shift in foreign policy and trade focus from Europe to Asia, including general tariff reductions and the promotion of an Asia-Pacific free trade area by the year 2020.

This, then, is the young country we shall examine—in its transition from wild frontier land to modern industrialized nation, and in the transformation this has wrought on its people.

TERRAIN

Australia is the only nation to occupy an entire continent—albeit the smallest of the seven continents. Surrounded by the Indian Ocean and the South Pacific, it is also an island—of 2,966,136 square miles (7,682,300 sq. km).

The island/continent lies southeast of the Asian landmass, bordered on the north by the Timor Sea, beyond which lie the islands of Papua New Guinea and Indonesia—the closest neighbors. To the east, the Coral Sea separates Australia from the island chain called the Solomon Islands, and the Tasman Sea separates it from New Zealand. On the west lies the Indian Ocean.

The sixth largest country on Earth, Australia extends approximately 2,500 miles (approximately 4,000 km) from east to west, and 1,875 miles (3,000 km) from north to south. The highest point is Mount Kosciusko, at 7,310 feet (2,228 m); the lowest point is Lake Eyre, at 39 feet (12 m) below sea level.

From east to west, Australia has four main geographical regions. The eastern lowland plain stretches from Cape York Peninsula in the north to the city of Melbourne in the south. Much of this area is forested. A few miles off the northern shore is the Great Barrier Reef, the largest coral reef in the world, which runs 1,200 miles (1,900 km) along the coast. On the southern part of the plain are the cities of Brisbane, Sydney, Canberra, and Melbourne—and Hobart in Tasmania.

The Eastern Highlands is a ridge of hills and

mountains that separate the lowlands from the interior. It includes the tropical mountain hinterland of Queensland, the hills of New England, the Blue Mountains, the Australian Alps in New South Wales and Victoria, and the mountains that dominate most of Tasmania.

West of the highlands lie the central plains. This is a region of dry depressions, or basins, the largest of which, the Great Artesian Basin, extends from the Gulf of Carpentaria in the north to the mouth of the Murray River in the south—the largest inland drainage system in the world.

The Western Plateau covers the western part of the continent with rocky ridges and plains, and large, forbidding deserts (the Great Sandy, the Gibson, the Great Victoria, and the Tanami). In the north, jungle and swamps cover Arnhem Land on the shore of the Gulf of Carpentaria. In the south, the Nullarbor (meaning "no trees") Plain borders the Great Australian Bight.

CLIMATE

Remember that Australia lies in the Southern Hemisphere, with seasons that are opposite those in the north—July is the middle of winter and January the peak of summer. Most of Australia is warm and dry, the southern part being the most comfortable, with temperatures in Melbourne averaging 48°F (9°C) in its July winter to 77°F (25°C) in January. Adelaide is similar, Perth a warmer. Temperatures in Darwin average 77°F (25°C) in July and 86°F (30°C) in January. The interior of Australia often reaches 100°F (38°C) and can go as high as 115°F (46°C).

The largest city, Sydney, has a subtropical climate, warm to hot and wet in summer, up to 95°F (35°C) and mild, dry winters, up to 77°F (25°C). Canberra's temperatures average 68°F (20°C) in January and 42°F (6°C) in July.

Northern Australia (beyond the Tropic of Capricorn) is subject to an extreme tropical wet/dry weather pattern. What this means is that from November to April there are torrential downpours, monsoonal storms, and high humidity in the city of Darwin and the northern cities and towns of Queensland.

Rainfall is lowest in the center (about 40 percent of the continent is desert), with less than 10 inches (25 cm) per year. Sheep and cattle stations (ranches) are found on the edges of these deserts. Crops mostly grow where the rainfall exceeds 10 inches (25 cm). Rainfall is greatest in the northeast tropical rainforest areas, with upwards of 59 inches (150 cm). In the south, Tasmania and Victoria receive more than 30 inches (76 cm), Adelaide and Perth less.

There is little that is ordinary about Australia. The extremes in climate from torrential rain to disastrous drought, and the ever-present threat of bushfires, along with the isolation of the continent for fifty million years, have combined to promote the country's rich and diverse native fauna and flora. Kangaroos of various sizes and colors, wallabies, and other oddities, such as the kookaburra, koala, platypus, echidna, galah, and many of the brightly colored parrots, are be found naturally nowhere else in the world. The ubiquitous Australian gum tree, or eucalyptus, which is dependent on bushfires for its survival and propagation, has been exported for use over much of the world, generally because of its thirst: its deep tap roots help to drain swamps and marshland.

AUSTRALIA'S ABORIGINES

It should be noted that Australia's Aboriginal peoples were not a single group of people. They were made up of at least six hundred widely scattered language groups. Some groups shared some beliefs, customs, and technological and cultural practices—the result of trade, intermarriage, and complex family connections— but there were also great differences between the groups. Even today, the Aboriginal population refers to itself as made up of many "peoples," or "nations," and it is common to talk about the Aboriginal Peoples of Australia when referring to them historically.

The Dreamtime

The Australian Aboriginal creation myths tell of "The Dreamtime," a time before history, when legendary, totemic Ancestral Beings sang the world into existence, and in doing so created the world and everything in it— plants, animals, landscape features, humans, and the customs and laws of those humans. Stories of the Dreamtime vary greatly from tribe to tribe, and from region to region, but the notion of the totemic ancestor is remarkably persistent. Images of these are to be found on the walls of rock shelters and caves in many parts of the country—the Aborigines are responsible for what is probably the world's greatest collection of rock art—and many different groups still use stories of the Dreamtime to explain the shape of a landform, the characteristic of a particular animal, or the existence of a particular law.

The Impact of the Settlers

At first the Aborigines showed little interest in assimilating into European society. Instead they expected the Europeans to continue their "Walkabout" and move on, or adopt the superior Aboriginal ways. But the tide rolled on, as it had done in the United States, in Canada, and wherever Europeans displaced indigenous people.

Aborigines and Europeans related to the land in completely opposing ways. The Aborigines were generally hunters and gatherers, although some groups were engaged in agricultural practices; the Europeans were farmers, who regarded the land as theirs for the taking because it was not being cultivated. The Aborigines were simply ignored by the Europeans, who declared Australia an empty and ownerless land, "*terra nullius.*" They were, as John Pilger put it in *A Secret Country*, considered not as human but rather as "part of the fauna." It was only in 1992 that the Australian High Court ruled that the Aborigines' title to the land had not been extinguished. Today, Australian Aborigines drive cars, or ride in trains, over the land they once trod so carefully.

The Aborigines realized, as the settlers kept coming, that the newcomers wanted to own the land, not to share it, and that they were here to stay—along with their fences, their missionaries to convert them, their politicians to interfere with them, their Community Service bureaucrats to take their children into care, their governments to

palm them off with rather useless tracts of land, and their alcohol. Many Aborigines exchanged work for food and lodgings, particularly on farms and in rural areas. Later came unemployment payouts and other cash benefits, meaning that many Aborigines had no real need to work, and there was ready access to alcohol. Successive governments, through a lack of understanding of how to cope with the problems of Aboriginals, contributed disaster along with benefit.

They had no immunity to the diseases the settlers introduced, and their numbers suffered accordingly. There were also murders. The most famous, perhaps, was the Myall Creek Massacre in 1838, when Aborigines—men, women, and children—were rounded up after some perceived wrongdoing (perhaps, as was often the case, they had taken a sheep to feed themselves), herded into a creek bed, and shot. We don't know how many there were, but there may have been hundreds. For this wanton killing of defenseless Aborigines, seven of the eleven whites accused were subsequently hanged. But such justice was not common.

From around the early 1900s a sort of cruel benevolence grew out of missionary interference and government ignorance, resulting in the white authorities' removal of Aboriginal children, particularly those of mixed blood (usually the result of white men's abuse of black women), from their families. This was an attempt to integrate them "for their own good" into white society.

Descendants from this "Stolen Generation," as it is called, were issued a national, public apology by the Prime Minister in 2008. While this was an important gesture of reconciliation, the fact remains that they are still searching for their roots, trying to discover who they really are.

There is now a great deal of concern for Aboriginal welfare. For most Australians, and for the visitor, this is a topic of great sensitivity and uncertainty. There is regret for what has been done, and for official ineptitude in the face of infant mortality rates, alcoholism, and family violence. While it is quite possible to live in Australia without getting to know any Aborigines—and, for those who live in the major cities, without actually seeing any—the problems of the Aborigines are always there. Most Australians abhor, and are embarrassed by, the fact of a disadvantaged underclass, marginalized and living on the fringes of society despite the spending of huge sums of money by recent governments. But there is also, among the ignorant and ill informed—mostly, but not entirely, outside the cities, and particularly in the north and northwest—a small, residual, hard core of racism that the Australians themselves call "redneck" ignorance.

The Aborigines Today
Many Aboriginal communities are dynamic and self-determining. This is particularly the case

where they have made successful claims to their traditional land, and now live on that land. Some communities support internationally recognized art centers where artists produce works that sell around the world, often for thousands of dollars. Other communities manage farmland, parkland, and mining leases.

Aborigines have been very successful activists, particularly over the last forty years. In 1967 they won the right to vote in what was the most unequivocal referendum held in Australia; in 1971 Aboriginal Neville Bonner was elected to the Senate; in 1972 Tent Embassy was set up outside Parliament to advance the cause of land rights (the returning of traditional lands); in 1992 a High Court decision, known as Mabo, rejected the notion of *terra nullius* and affirmed that Aboriginal people were in possession of the land prior to 1788; in the late 1990s the notion of Reconciliation (coming to terms with wrongs of the past as related to the treatment of Aborigines) was embraced by many Australians.

There are many highly successful Aboriginal people in Australian public life. They include:

- Noel Pearson (politician and activist); Lowitja O'Donohue (activist and senior public administrator, and former Australian of the Year).
- Cathy Freeman (an Olympic medallist), Adam Goode (football player and indigenous youth

advocate); Evonne Goolagong-Cawley, winner of seven tennis grand slams and first indigenous person to win Wimbledon.
- Deborah Mailman (actor); David Gulpilil (actor); Ernie Dingo (actor and television personality).
- Singers Geoffrey Gurrumul Yunupingu and Jessica Mauboy; and Albert Namatjira—Australia's foremost aboriginal artist.

Nevertheless, you would be well advised to approach the subject of the Aboriginal Peoples with great caution. Read about it, and try to understand. Ask questions, by all means, and listen.

THE AUSTRALIANS

The arrival of the First Fleet of eleven ships from Britain in 1788, carrying over thirteen hundred people, began the influx of different cultures to Australia. First came English seamen and soldiers, along with English and Irish convicts. These were followed by free settlers, mostly from England—ethnically and culturally Celtic and Anglo-Saxon—and a significant number of Chinese, who arrived to try their luck on the goldfields during the great gold rush of the 1850s. Between 1851 and 1860 the rate of immigration was fifty thousand per annum. The immigrants and the Aborigines mostly went their separate ways.

Postwar immigration brought a wide variety of Europeans from war-torn Europe—six million since 1945. Australia implemented a policy of free passage for United Kingdom residents, and assisted passage for ex-servicemen from the British Isles, the USA, the Netherlands, Norway, France, Belgium, and Denmark. From 1950 to 1960 economic and humanitarian events also opened the gates to Germany, Turkey, Yugoslavia, Chile (after Allende), and Indochina (after the Vietnam war).

Since 1960 the population of Australia has more than doubled (from 10 million in 1960 to 23 million today), mainly due to a steady influx of immigrants from over 120 countries. The top ten source countries of migrants today are, in order: India, China, the UK, the Philippines, Pakistan, Ireland (the Irish Republic), South Africa, Nepal, and Malaysia.

This mixture of ethnic and cultural origins has resulted in the most multicultural mixture of people in the world. They call themselves Australians.

GOVERNMENT AND POLITICS

Australia is divided into six states (New South Wales, Queensland, South Australia, Victoria,

Western Australia, and Tasmania) and two territories (the Northern Territory and the Australian Capital Territory—in which is located the Federal Capital, Canberra).

Until late in the nineteenth century, these areas were separately governed British colonies. In the late 1800s, Australians realized the advantages to be gained by becoming one unified nation. A constitution was drawn up and approved by the British Parliament in 1901, reflecting the country's British origin and based on the Westminster system of government.

The King or Queen of England is the official head of state, and has formal power but little direct authority over Australian laws and government. The Governor-General is the monarch's representative.

As in the UK and Canada, the Prime Minister is the leader of the party that has the most members elected to the parliament, which is divided into upper and lower houses. The lower house, the House of Representatives, has 150 members elected for a three-year term and is essentially the legislative body. Only this house can propose and pass bills that affect government money and spending. The upper house, the Senate, has seventy-six members—twelve from each state and two from each territory. Those from states serve six-year terms; those from territories serve three-year terms.

There are several political parties in Australia, each embracing a political philosophy different from the others. This difference is actually more noticeable between minor parties, such as the Greens, Family First, and the Shooters and Fishers Party, and the Democrats, and between them and

the two main parties, than between the two main parties. These are the Labor Party (with a history arising from its roots in trade unions and blue-collar workers), and the Liberal/National Country Party coalition (with a history arising from roots in the farming community and industrialists and white-collar workers). Voting for these two tends to be within the range of 47 to 53 percent. They have become close in ideology. Some of the smaller parties have a narrow agenda and, despite being a motley crew, have in recent years held the important balance of power in minority OR coalition governments.

Politics is the subject of much discussion in Australia, at least in part because voting is compulsory, but it is interesting to note that it is not the voting that is compulsory, but visiting the polling booth to have your name crossed off. What this means, of course, is that a person can simply attend, and then either fail to fill out a voting form or provide a "donkey vote" (mark the paper in a humorous or even obscene way). The important thing is that the number of donkey votes is insignificant. Australians take their voting seriously, and in the main know exactly what they are voting for.

"Talk-back" radio is bigger in Australia, perhaps, than anywhere else in the world, and many people listen avidly; particularly people in regional areas, workers who can have the radio on in factories, garages, offices, and stay-at-home parents. Listeners are kept very much up to date on current affairs and politics.

Regarding political debate, as a visitor you would be well advised to question and listen, but you should, of course, be careful when expressing opinions on local politics. Where you can make a contribution is in a discussion of the politics of your own country. You might be surprised by how much Australians know about world affairs. The news in Australia, in the newspapers, on the radio, and on television, and particularly through SBS—Special Broadcasting Services—contains much more overseas news than is generally found in other countries. The Australians like to keep up with what is going on.

Historical Snapshot

1770 Captain Cook lands at Botany Bay, and calls the eastern coastline New South Wales.

1788 Captain Arthur Phillip and the First Fleet arrive, with convicts.

1793 The first free settlers arrive.

1803 Matthew Flinders circumnavigates the mainland.

1840 Abolition of convict transportation to New South Wales.

1851 Gold discovered in Victoria and New South Wales.

1897–8 New and separate Australian Constitution prepared.

1899 Constitution approved by ballot of the people.

1900 Federation of Australian Colonies—British approval. Melbourne becomes temporary capital of the new nation.

1901 January 1: Australia declared an independent Commonwealth within the British Empire. Local voting for local parliament.

1908 Canberra (midway between Melbourne and Sydney) chosen as the permanent Federal Capital.

1914 Australia enters First World War.

1915 More than 8,000 Australian soldiers lost in battle of Gallipoli in Turkey; 62,000 Australian lives lost in the First World War.

1920 QANTAS (Queensland and Northern Territory Aerial Services) founded.

1928 Royal Flying Doctor Service established.

1939 Australia enters the Second World War.

1942 Darwin bombed by the Japanese on February 19, 1943.

1947 Australian government buys all shares in QANTAS.

1956 Olympic Games held in Melbourne.

1965 Australian soldiers sent to the Vietnam conflict.

1967 Referendum sees 90 percent of Australians say "yes" to the right of Aborigines to vote.

1973 Opening of the Sydney Opera House.

1975 Governor-General John Kerr sacks Prime Minister Gough Whitlam.

1983 Australia II wins the America's Cup yacht race.

1993 Native Title Act passed to help Aborigines press land claims.

1996 A Liberal-National Coalition Government led by John Howard won the general election and was re-elected in 1998, 2001 and 2004, enacting several reforms, including changes in the taxation and industrial relations systems.

2000 Olympic Games held in Sydney.

2001 Australian forces are deployed in Afghanistan and the Persian Gulf.

2002 Bombs detonated near popular tourist nightclubs in Bali by Islamist terrorists kill 202, including 88 Australians.

2003 Australia provides combat forces to support the USA invasion of Iraq.

2004 Australia and the USA sign a Free Trade Agreement.

2006 Australian Forces are deployed to East Timor.

2007 The Labor Party led by Kevin Rudd was elected with an agenda to reform.

Australia's industrial relations system, climate change policies, and health and education sectors.

2008 Australia ends combat operations in Iraq.

2009 Bushfires in the state of Victoria claim over 200 lives.

The withdrawal of Australian forces from Iraq is completed.

2010 Julia Gillard replaces Kevin Rudd as Prime Minister following a Labor Party leadership tussle.

China overtakes the USA as Australia's largest export partner for trade.

2013 Tony Abbott, leader of the Liberal/National Coalition becomes Prime Minister after his party wins the general election.

2014 Australia signs Free Trade Agreements with Japan and South Korea.

VALUES *&* ATTITUDES

"FAIR DINKUM"

Australia is an ethnic melting pot—but it wasn't always that way. Beliefs like being "fair dinkum" (being honest, up-front, a person who keeps to his or her word) go back to the pioneering days. That is not to say that the phrase is inappropriate today, because immigrants were quick to pick it up. The fact is that those immigrant converts to what epitomized the Australian way of life (or what Australians like to think is peculiar to their way of life) seemed to take it up with a new intensity. No more "fair dinkum Aussies" exist than those who left the postwar awfulness of Europe for sunnier shores.

Equally, it wasn't long before Australians noticed that these new arrivals worked a bit harder than they were accustomed to themselves, and that they prospered. For example, they observed that those from the Mediterranean built themselves very big brick houses with lots of tiles and marble, and balustrades on verandas and staircases. At first this gave rise to some envy-based criticism from a more laid-back Australian working community. This was fairly quickly replaced by a desire that they, too, should have a big house with all these trimmings.

It is, perhaps, fair to say that early immigrants brought with them, and inculcated into Australia, a new, or at least a stronger, work ethic.

WORKING TO LIVE VERSUS LIVING TO WORK

During the 1990s, an Australian who worked for an American company was visited by a senior executive from the USA. The visitor asked him to arrange for the management team to join him for a breakfast meeting on Sunday morning. "Bloody hell!" the Australian thought (see Communication Styles, page 157), knowing that there was no way the team would give up their golf tee-off time, an early swim or jog, or simply a relaxed breakfast with the family—just for a *meeting!*

The Australian, a quick thinker, said: "It probably wouldn't be a good idea. I don't think they would be too impressed about missing church. And to some of them, even the *idea* of working on the Sabbath. . ."

The meeting was scheduled for Monday morning!

It is not that Australians do not work long hours (a myth perpetuated by many writers), but that other countries work even longer hours. According to recent OECD (Organization for Economic Cooperation and Development) figures, over the first decade of the 2000s, Australia dropped from ranking 3rd to 19th in the numbers of hours worked by industrialized nations, with the average work week decreasing from 35 to 33 hours.

The real issue here is not a problem with the number of hours worked, but the majority of Australians do not happily give up their "living" time. That's why they work: to live—to enjoy the weather, the beaches, the sports, and the socializing.

Should you gain employment in Australia, you will be expected (by other workers) to work the same hours as they do.

"MATESHIP"

You will notice a form of address that is used by many Australian men toward all males: "mate." "G'day, mate;" "What can I get you, mate?" This is simply a casual, cheerful greeting, with no great overtones of friendship.

True "mateship" was traditionally something quite different; in fact it was almost mystical. It grew out of a feeling of fellowship between men who were facing or had lived through extreme or difficult conditions or great adversity together. It was the brotherhood that came from the sharing of any significant experience, such as fighting together in wartime. As one old soldier said, "The blokes in the trenches were not all friends, but they were all mates. We knew we would all go over the top of the trenches together." At a later stage, perhaps, mateship could come from a different kind of adversity, such as making sure a drunken friend gets home safely, or providing

physical or emotional support for a broken down car—or marriage! Aussies think, "Only a real mate would do that." While "mateship" used to be the exclusive domain of men, this rather gruff term of respect (and endearment) is occasionally today used when addressing women—a sign of acceptance and expression of gender equality—Australian style!

Australians inherited from their British forebears a capacity for self-mockery. However, many fell for the Pioneer image that is associated with the mateship ethos, and still like to see themselves in the *Crocodile Dundee* image (referring to actor Paul Hogan's hit movies of 1985 and 1988); they wear bush hats; some even wear "digger" (Australian for "soldier")-style army hats with the brim turned up on one side; and wear the iconic bushman's "driza-bone" long oilcloth coats—even to pop out for a coffee in suburban Melbourne on a rainy day.

Nowadays this kind of exclusiveness has made mateship seem rather old-fashioned. It is also worth noting that the term "mate" is sometimes used ironically, to indicate relationships—such as may occur in criminal or political circles—that are not necessarily upfront and honest.

The reality of mateship today is that it comes to the fore in times of crisis, and is manifested as a general sense of cooperation and a "can-do" attitude among all Australians, men and women. In the bushfires that regularly afflict Australia every summer thousands of volunteer firefighters (many of them women) simply leave their jobs, don their uniforms, and stand side by side for days at a time, trying to protect the property of others. Australians are proud and independent, but they come together in a crisis, lending a hand to help their mates.

"CULTURAL CRINGE" AND "TALL POPPIES"

These two Aussie characteristics are worth exploring—even though these attitudes are both on the wane. There was a time when

Australians thought that anything American, British, or European must be better than its Australian counterpart. Probably this was the case, many years ago. This self-deprecation gave birth to a kind of social embarrassment, or so-called "cultural cringe."

At about the time of the Melbourne Olympics, in 1956, when visitors exclaimed how well the games worked, how well Australia did, how interesting the museums and art galleries were, and how much they enjoyed the theater, Australians began to see themselves as having caught up, culturally. Unfortunately, this perceived success in the arts, as well as in moviemaking, in pop music, and, above all, in sport, resulted in overconfidence, evident in some Australians, particularly when overseas. Maybe a bit of "cringe" was not such a bad thing.

In days long gone by, many Australians liked to think of themselves as Little Aussie Battlers— working-class people struggling against upper-class bosses. However, when one of those battlers "made it" by achieving success, fame, or money, he became "one of them Tall Poppies"—and Tall Poppies needed to be cut down to size. Today, however, it is fine, even admirable, to achieve success, provided that you do not forget your mates or your beginnings.

RELIGION

In a recent census, in response to the optional question on religion, approximately 61 percent of the population were found to be Christian (a decline since the previous census a decade ago), the rest were made up of different Protestant denominations. Among the fastest growing reported religious affiliations are Buddhism (2.5 percent), Islam (2.2 percent), and Hinduism (1.3 percent). What is perhaps most interesting is that 23 percent stated that they had no religion, or gave no answer.

RETURN OF THE JEDI?

To illustrate many Australians' rather irreverent attitude to religion: when answering the question on religion in the 2001 Census, 70,509 Australians (some 0.37 percent) wrote "Jedi" or a variant, in response to an email campaign claiming (mistakenly) that if 8,000 people said they followed the Jedi religion in the forthcoming census, the country would have to recognize it officially.

Generally, church attendance in Australia is falling quite dramatically. Religion is one of those sacred cows that are more the butt of humor than the subject of serious discussions. While attitudes to right and wrong at a social, moral level have their foundation in Judeo-Christian values—for example, a reluctance to steal, lie, or cheat (or at least to be caught doing so)—these are not generally seen as religious mores. Giving someone "a fair go," and "looking after your mate" would probably be more readily given reasons for doing the right thing.

Overall, religion is not taken very seriously by the masses, and rarely would workmates at any level need to know, or even care, what religion the others are.

However, as with anywhere in the world, you would need to know your company very well indeed before entering into critical debate on the subject.

HUMOR

It is an article of faith in Australia that all visitors must be able to take a joke. Learn to laugh at yourself, your country, and so on— and if you really want to be a social hit, tell jokes against yourself, your country, and the way you speak.

Nothing is sacred. There is almost nothing that cannot be laughed at. Particularly good things to poke fun at are religion and religious hierarchy, politics and politicians, Australians (provided you are Australian—Australian humor is often very self-deprecating), Poms

(British people—even weak jokes will do), and all sacred cows. The important things of life are taken very lightly. Sport, however, is taken very seriously!

The Australian humorist best-known internationally is probably still Barry Humphries, who has

the distinction of convincing most Americans
that she is Dame Edna Everage—for real.

As an illustration of Australia's tongue
in cheek approach to describing what is
important to the average Aussie, a list of
'unAustralian' behaviours and attitudes
regularly circulates on the Internet. Here
are some extracts:

IT'S UNAUSTRALIAN:

- Not knowing the second verse to
  Advance Australia Fair.
- Not knowing there is a second verse to
  Advance Australia Fair.
- To leave the pub before you've bought a
  round (or "shout") of drinks.
- To live in England for two years and
  never to go out of London.
- To not to add an "o" to your mate's first
  name (unless he's called Antonio, in
  which case you call him "Ant").
- Not owning thongs (for the feet).

ATTITUDES TOWARD OTHERS

Most Australians are saddened by the plight
of those Aboriginal people whose numbers,
culture, and way of life were—and continue to
be—blighted by European settlement. A few

racist bigots ignore the successful among them and blame the Aborigines for failure to assimilate and for perpetuating the high incidences of alcoholism, family violence, and disease in their communities. However, Australians overwhelmingly supported the Government's 2008 national apology statement to its indigenous community, specifically to the "stolen generations" for its policy of forced assimilation and, generally for its misguided efforts to impose culture change on to the country's original owners.

It is, of course, difficult, if not impossible, to lump together the attitudes of all Australians. "All Australians" includes those of Continental European immigrant stock; those who are of English stock and are actually proud of it; those republicans who are of English stock and want to forget it; those of Aboriginal stock who just want to be recognized; and those of Asian stock, who must be vastly bewildered by all of the above. But the following may help you, the visitor, just a little bit, to understand some general attitudes.

Most Australians have nothing against the British (although you will sometimes hear the words "Brit" or "Brits" used disparagingly). That is, they have nothing against the Welsh, the Scottish, or the Irish. They may, however, have something against the English.

In the early postwar years there was a great deal of immigration from England. Many English folk were placed in some pretty awful new towns (Elizabeth in South Australia was one), far from the sea and the beaches they saw as typifying Australia. They gained a reputation for "whingeing" (grumbling) that things were not the same as they were back home. Many Australians offered to pay for their return. These English immigrants were given the name "Poms" (origin obscure— though a popularly held belief is that it is an acronym of 'Prisoner of His/Her Majesty), and, in particular, "whingeing Poms."

Yes, it *was* a bit like that. Today, most of the younger Australians have forgotten why the Poms simply have to be the butt of all jokes. It's a bit rough on the new immigrants— the older ones have learned to give it back.

The slang term to describe the British— "Poms"—is derisory yet affectionate and, with changing demographics, somewhat dated— nowadays mostly reserved to describe the opposition in a Test (cricket) Match, or sunburnt tourists on Bondi beach. Despite the rise in republican sentiment, a 1999 referendum which proposed replacing the monarchy with a republic was narrowly defeated; however, given that immigrants are increasingly from Asia rather than "the old country," an Australian republic seems to be just a question of time. In early 2015, in a "taking of the pulse" on Monarchist vs Republican sentiment, the Prime Minister Tony Abbott's personal decision to make the Queen's husband, the Duke of Edinburgh, a "Knight of the Order of Australia" was met with derision ("doesn't the bloke have enough gongs—awards and titles?") and outrage, rocking Abbott's leadership as people assessed him to be "out of touch" with the Australian people on this—and other —issues.

Australians have generally liked Continental Europeans because of their significant contributions, such as providing the labor for iconic infrastructure projects, like the Snowy Mountains hydroelectric scheme— and not least because they introduced welcome culinary alternatives to the English imports of overcooked meat and two veg!

Australians like Asians because they are gentle, industrious, their children are well behaved and high achieving, and because of Yum Cha, Nasi Goreng, lemongrass, sambals, satay, sushi…

And most Australians believe the Yanks saved them from Japanese invasion in the Second World War.

Despite Australia's tolerance, however, the issue of refugees is an extremely sensitive one.

A great many people believe that asylum seekers should not be admitted at all; conversely many Australians are ashamed of the treatment of political refugees—particularly their long-term detention in off-shore detention centers. Visitors should tread very carefully here.

Since the terrorist attacks in the USA on September 11, 2001, and Bali in 2004 by Islamic fundamentalists, some followers of Islam in Australia have reported incidents of verbal abuse and a sense of marginalization. Until then, Asian Muslims who wore Islamic dress were accepted with no more than the curious glance that may be given to anyone whose appearance is strikingly different, but terrorism has changed that.

A great deal of effort is being made by the government and religious and other bodies to allay fears, which are to be found at the root of any prejudice. Most Australians abhor what they refer to as "redneck" racism.

Attitudes toward Women
Australian women from all states (though, it should be noted, not indigenous men or women) won the right to vote by Federation in 1901—ahead of the women's suffrage movement in Europe. After such an auspicious start, the Australian feminist movement has lagged behind its European and North

American counterparts, despite significant legislation promoting gender equality. While women today outnumber men in number of undergraduate and postgraduate degrees attained, there is still a lack of gender balance in leadership positions across the board—and particularly in the boardroom.

Yes—Australia has experienced its first female Governor General (Quentin Bryce) and Prime Minister, the latter—Julie Gillard—attracting worldwide headlines lecturing the leader of the opposition on misogyny during a parliamentary exchange.

Attitudes to Each Other

Australians' attitudes to each other have changed little. There is still a strong sense of egalitarianism, and it is true that you can be talking to someone in a pub, or at a dinner party, or a barbecue, and be quite unaware that they are very important or very rich. D. H. Lawrence observed of Australia, that "whereas some people felt 'better off' than others, nobody felt better than anyone else." And a British officer is known to have remarked of Australian soldiers that they "only saluted the officers that they liked."

There is a general dislike of those who exercise authority where this is felt to be undeserved or inappropriate, and this attitude is also seen in a frequent breaking of petty, unpopular, or seemingly pointless rules.

And you, the visitor, or new arrival? You will find that, if you keep your sense of humor and show a lively interest in the land and the people, Australians will take to you. As a visitor to their homes you will be warmly welcomed—as long as you keep quiet about being very wealthy, very educated, or very important.

chapter three

THE AUSTRALIANS AT HOME

HOME OWNERSHIP

"A home of my own" has for years been the great Australian dream. For around 68 percent of Australians the dream has come true, and they own their own home, or the mortgage servicing it. But it is becoming more difficult. House prices have risen disproportionately in relation to incomes over recent years. Housing developments around the cities have engulfed much of the available land, and new-home buyers have been driven further away from the city centers, creating huge suburban sprawls around Sydney and Melbourne. There is a shortage of land closer to the cities and their amenities, and this has contributed to the great increase in the building of high-rise apartment complexes (apartments are called "flats units" in Australia). These generally cluster near the city, along train lines and bus routes, and near the beaches.

HOUSE STYLES

When the settlers built towns and cities in the late eighteenth and early nineteenth centuries, they built homes that resembled the ones they had left behind. Fine examples of Victorian architecture can be found in older and mostly inner-city suburban areas, such as Paddington in Sydney, Fitzroy in Melbourne, and in many country towns. Still admired by some, they sell at high prices. However, thin and squeezed together as they were, they must have looked out of place in Australia's open landscapes, and they failed to take advantage of the climate, with its abundant sunshine and balmy breezes.

If you want to see what the great Australian houses of the nineteenth century looked like, any travel agent or hotel front desk will give you information. If you are in Sydney, see Vaucluse House, after which you might enjoy drinking coffee in nearby Double Bay (known by locals as *Double Pay*), and watching fashionable Sydneysiders go by. If you are in Melbourne,

visit Como House in the fashionable suburb
of South Yarra.

A train ride from the city of Sydney to
Parramatta, heading west, will enable you
to see older suburban housing styles.

In Hornsby, on the north shoreline, you will
see more modern housing. In Melbourne, taking
the Epping line to Clifton Hill, and changing to
return to Jolimont, will provide opportunities
to see similar varieties of housing. At Jolimont
you can visit the famous Melbourne Cricket
Ground and take a short walk back to the city
via Fitzroy Gardens (where you can see Captain
Cook's Cottage) and the beautiful Royal Botanical
Gardens.

Later architects designed low, sprawling,
ranch-type houses that were better suited
to the hot, dry weather. These were single-
story detached houses—known elsewhere as

bungalows—set on large blocks of land. This basic six-room home is still the benchmark. Designs changed: continuously in vogue are historic (and imitation) "Federation" homes, charming colonial buildings with porches and verandas all the way around, supported by pillars and with elaborately lacy wrought-iron work.

Other popular housing styles include Spanish and Mediterranean designs; the Queenslander—a large, timbered, tropical house set high above ground level to allow air to circulate; and organic yet sleek timber and stone structures.

Until quite recently, standard houses were traditionally built on quarter-acre (approximately one-tenth of a hectare) lots, and in more expensive areas the lots were bigger. As land has become scarcer, local councils have allowed smaller housing blocks—newer blocks are about half the size of the old standard.

Most living in modern Australian homes revolves around a kitchen-dining room, family room, rumpus or games room, patio, or veranda. At weekends there is a move to the backyard, by the swimming pool or barbecue. The kitchen is often of open-plan design, allowing for a great deal of social life. As a visitor you will often find yourself there, chatting with whoever is doing the cooking, and having a drink and pre-dinner appetizers.

Some older houses have formal rooms for formal occasions. You may find yourself sitting

in a rarely used "lounge room" and, if invited
for dinner, moving to a separate dining room.

Most modern homes will have more than one
"loo" (WC, toilet, lavatory) and hand basin. It is
usual, if you are there for dinner, to be offered
these facilities in terms of "using the bathroom"
or "washing your hands." If this offer is not
forthcoming, it is perfectly acceptable to ask,
"May I use the bathroom?"

SUBURBAN LIVING

The southern capitals have cool to cold winters,
barely above freezing point at times. Sydney and
even Brisbane have cool winters. Towns in the
center of Australia, like Alice Springs, can get
quite cold. So despite the fact that you are going
to sunny Australia you will need warm "woollies,"
and maybe a raincoat. Houses are mostly heated
in some way in winter—not so often these days
by crackling log fires, more often by portable
electric or oil heaters, and occasionally by air-
conditioning. Cooling comes with reverse-cycle
air conditioning. Oddly enough, in the Eastern
States there is less cooling than heating; although
some houses do have evaporative air-cooling
systems, some simply rely on fans. Most offices,
restaurants, and shopping centers are air-
conditioned.

Local councils provide libraries and council
offices where residents can find information on

building requirements and so on, and pay council taxes. These cover the cost of garbage removal (by big wheeled bins, mechanically emptied into trucks once a week, usually keeping separate paper, plastic, and kitchen waste).

Suburban living is, generally, in no way personally dangerous. A few suburbs are exceptions, and are to be avoided, and a visitor will be made aware of these exceptions. Very few of the assaults that occur are random—they are generally personal or gang related. Throughout most of the sprawling suburbs it is safe to walk the streets, and many health-conscious folk take nightly jogs, though it may be more sensible, as in most places, to do so with a friend.

There is one big exception to this matter of safety. You personally are generally safe; but your household effects are less safe. Most robberies are committed in daylight, while the owners are out or away, so when Australians leave their houses nowadays they lock all the doors and windows. (Less than thirty years ago, people rarely locked their house doors when going out).

GARDENING

Gardening is an Australian obsession. The size of the housing lot means that there will be a front yard, a backyard, and a driveway down one side. The front yard is a canvas on which most Australians feel the need to paint—verdant lawns splashed with the brilliance of native flora, such as grevilleas, banksias, kangaroo's paw, and bottle brush, and imported roses, chrysanthemums, and dahlias. Many Australians spend many hours of the weekend digging, planting, pruning, weeding, and, most of all, watering. The front yard represents the individual image that the householder wants to present to the world. Australians care, too, about upholding the standards in the neighborhood, in terms of keeping the garden neat and tidy—and bringing their dustbins in promptly after garbage pick-up!

When visiting Australians at home, it is important to be aware of the pride they feel in their efforts to make their place beautiful, in most cases particularly their garden. Commenting on it, and showing interest, will win you many hearts and will ensure you are welcome.

The Victa Mower

In 1952, in Sydney, Mervyn Victor Richardson welded a peach tin to a miniature motor, filled it with gasoline, and attached it to a lawn mower with rotary blades. By the mid 1990s, six million Australians were mowing with a Victa.

Tools are signs of the do-it-yourself disease (DIY), which most suburban householders catch. Australian men and women are, on the whole, very handy and practical. DIY is a large industry in Australia and, to many people, heaven is the local DIY hardware emporium—vast areas stacked with every conceivable fixing thing, or replacement thing, from washers, taps, and baths, to garden sheds and "bar-b-ques."

One such "barbie" will be in the backyard—usually a gas-fired one, although a few stalwarts still have a brick-and-hotplate structure that burns wood. These traditionalists will probably show you how a handful of gum (eucalyptus) leaves thrown on the fire adds to the flavor of the meat. Try this if you use one of the many barbecues available to the public in suburban parks (run by the local councils—wood supplied), or if you are in the bush (in the country, or in scrubland on the side of the road), or at a beach. Many Australians take a portable barbecue on a country drive instead of a traditional picnic lunch. You need to be sure in summer that high temperatures have not brought about a ban on open fires. Breaking the ban carries large fines. (There is more on being invited to a barbecue in Chapter 6, Time Out.)

SCHOOLS AND SCHOOLING

Australia offers a free public education system to its over three million children. The system has three levels: elementary (from six to twelve years of age), secondary (from age twelve to fifteen or sixteen), and tertiary (university level). The names given to the levels, and the ages, vary a little from state to state. Many parents send their children to preschools or kindergartens from the age of three or four. There are a number of expensive private schools, many of them religious institutions, most of which do not limit students to followers of their religion. These provide for more than a million students. Since 2009 children have been required by law to continue their education until seventeen, either at school or through some combination of vocational training and employment.

Australia has an educated population, in that almost every Australian over the age of ten can read and write. However, there is concern that many Australian seventeen-year-olds do not continue with their education, whereas Japanese seventeen-year-olds nearly all go on to university. Asian influence is considerable, because of the large numbers of Asian students being sent to study at Australian universities—and the large number of Asian families immigrating—who are inculcated with an extremely strong study ethic. In fact, Asians achieve a disproportionate percentage of top places in Australia's university entrance exams.

Children who live in the outback (in the country, and far away from towns), on sheep or cattle stations many miles inland, are often too far away from any school to attend classes. To cater to them, the Australian government created Schools of the Air. These schools send lessons and homework through the mail and use two-way radio to enable students and teachers to communicate during regular school hours. You can visit a School of the Air at Broken Hill, an interesting old mining town in the far west of New South Wales. For further information see: www.schoolair-p.schools. nsw.edu.au/contact-us.

THE SCHOOL YEAR

The dates of school terms vary between states. As a rough guide, they tend to run as follows:

- First term: end of January to the first week of April.
- Second term: end of April to the end of June.
- Third term: end of July to the end of September.
- Fourth term: first week of October to the second week of December.

SHOPS AND SERVICES

As a broad generalization, shops open at 8:30 or 9:00 a.m. and close about 5:00 or 5:30 p.m. Bakers, delicatessens, and newspaper shops open earlier; flower shops, cake shops, and liquor stores close later. Many shops close later in the evening, especially those located in shopping centers with supermarkets, because many of these have extended hours. Some are open until midnight;

others are open twenty-four hours. Banks are usually open from 9:30 a.m. until either 4.00 or 5:00 p.m. on Fridays, and some branches open now on Saturday mornings.

Supermarkets have replaced most corner shops. Many more are located in vast, one-stop shopping centers alongside all the traditional shops and department stores, cinemas, restaurants, other food outlets (especially the multi-cuisine food halls discussed in Chapter 6), government departments such as Medicare (government medical fund), post offices, and gas stations. In the huge parking garages attached to these shopping centers, take a careful note of exactly where you have parked, identifying your space or the area by level, color, or number.

TV AND RADIO

Many Australians watch a lot of television—children particularly, and very young children more particularly. Some mothers will confess to using the TV as a babysitter, usually in the late afternoon when they are busy preparing the evening meal. The ABC (Australian Broadcasting Commission) caters to this by showing some very good programs, educational as well as entertaining, for children at these times. Adults vary in their viewing, from those who have the TV on in the kitchen-dining area, to those who restrict it to the family room. Most Australians have digital and cable TV, and "binge" on "box sets" or download their favourite TV series.

Of interest to you as a visitor or new arrival is Channel SBS (Special Broadcasting Services), which describes itself as: "the voice and vision of multicultural Australia." It is—broadcasting the most comprehensive world news in English every night, and some foreign language news and current affairs programs during the day. Of added value to visitors from overseas (as well as locals) are current affairs programs such as SBS's "Insight" and ABC's 7:30 p.m. "Report and Q&A."

The majority of homes now have a computer, which is taking over some of the time school-age children used to spend on watching TV.

As in many other countries, collective activities such as meal times or TV viewing often feature various family members constantly checking in with iPhones and iPads—unless house rules about use of electronic devices prevail!

There is a quantity of "talk," or "talkback," radio, in which listeners are invited to call the radio station and give their views on news, politics, or any subject that interests them. These programs have half-hourly news broadcasts, plus interviews with politicians (who recognize the broad reach of talk radio across Australia), medical practitioners, lawyers, doctors, teachers, and all experts in their fields. In this way visitors and new arrivals can learn what interests or concerns some Australians—if they can put up with the mix of polarizing views and inane banter!

chapter four

MAKING FRIENDS

First, you have to meet them! Australians are to be found in pubs and clubs, in coffee shops, on the beach, at sporting events, at work, and in the variety of other places people might gather.

WHERE TO FIND THEM

Pubs

A pub may also be called a "hotel," or even "the local" (as in "meet you at the hotel," "see you in the pub," "let's try the local"). Some of the city pubs and a few suburban pubs are quite good, offering reasonably attractive bars, bistros for a meal, and beer gardens for outside eating and drinking. (Children are allowed into beer gardens, but not into the bars.) Beer gardens with bistros are also popular spots in the afternoons and on warm evenings—to meet old friends and to find new ones.

Seek out the pubs that have entertainment—comedians, bands, singers, and the like. They are good fun, and good places to observe and meet the locals. Melbourne is particularly well known for its comedy and live music scene entertainment in pubs.

Some other pubs are not so attractive, with noise from the TAB (Totaliser Agency Board, which enables betting on most sports) drowning the conversation. Customers combine drinking with betting on the horse races, listening to the race broadcast, and shouting encouragement to horses and jockeys. Beachside pubs can be very rowdy, but offer entertainment and a good time, especially on hot weekends. Every city has quieter, more sophisticated pubs downtown, in which it is possible to sit in comfortable surroundings, often with a city or harbor view, and where you will pay a little more for a relaxing drink or two.

Cafés and Bars

There are plenty of informal cafés and bars in towns, the cafés often serving alcohol as well as the bars. There are café/bar precincts, such as Darlinghurst in Sydney, and Brunswick Street in Melbourne. Cafés and bars are relaxed and friendly, and are very popular with all age ranges, but particularly younger professional people.

Clubs

Mostly in New South Wales—these you must see! Many of these were established by sporting clubs (principally rugby league, see page 79) or branches of the RSL (Returned Soldiers League, see pages 75, 100). They have big, opulent buildings surrounded by lawn bowling greens and filled with poker machines (slot machines), bars, restaurants, gymnasiums, cinemas, and auditoriums for entertainment. They are not-for-profit organizations, and because of this are able to offer all their services cheaply—very cheaply.

A main dish such as Thai or Indian curries, pasta dishes, or the standard roast meats with vegetables, fish and chips, or pasta dishes are affordably priced. As a visitor to Australia, you will be admitted to any club free (carry some sort of identification), or you must live a certain distance, such as three miles (five kilometers) from the club. You fill in a form at the door. If you are staying in Australia for some time you can take out an annual membership, which can vary from $15 to $150.

There are also numerous "ethnic" clubs, for Greeks, Italians, Hungarians, Germans, and so on, though they tend to be less frequented by the younger generation.

Joining/Avoiding Clubs

It is handy to have one or two club memberships:
perhaps a Leagues (rugby) club and an RSL club.
Membership entitles you to entry to those clubs
anywhere in New South Wales, without the need
to prove that you are a visitor to Australia. They
offer affordable meals and drinks (cheaper than
at pubs) with many clubs enjoying prime spots
with stunning beach views. At your home club
you are also entitled to a reasonably cheap gym
membership, restaurant dining (not as cheap
as the club bistro, but still great value), and the
opportunity to join in a variety of sports.

Then why avoid them? Well, it is important to
be aware that the poker machines (slot machines)
subsidize everything in the club. They can be very
tempting for visitors, as some of the prizes (such
as automobiles) are quite staggering. Suffice it
to say that poker machine gambling is a serious
problem for some patrons. Each state has its
casinos, with poker machines, and they take huge
amounts of money daily, even hourly. It is known
that New South Wales club poker machines take
a big slice of the gambling, accounting for a 40
percent share of NSW's $3.2 billion of annual
gaming machine profits. So enjoy the clubs, but
beware of the "pokies."

Eating Places

There are many casual eating places in shopping
centers and tourist areas. They provide a great

variety of cuisines for large numbers of people, and you often share a table with others.

Beaches

The wonderful beaches offer much to visitors and locals alike, and tend to be packed, particularly on hot weekends. Visitors need to be careful when swimming or surfing. Stick to the rules (see pages 132–3). Apart from swimming, most beaches offer pubs, restaurants with a view, pleasant walks, street shopping, take-out food outlets, and picnic places in parks or on lawns.

Churches

The established Christian Churches offer immediate contact with people having similar interests. Or you can join one of the newer and increasingly popular evangelical churches.

(In these you will find instant recognition as a newcomer, and a warm welcome. The congregations in the established Churches might be a little slower to approach you, but eventually they will.) Similarly, mosques, synagogues, and temples for Hindus, Buddhists, and others are welcoming and offer friendship to new arrivals.

Sporting Events
All sporting events gather crowds—golf, tennis, racing, cricket, and, most of all, football—rugby (both league and union) and "Aussie Rules" (see Chapter 5, A God Named Sport). On a sunny day the atmosphere is fun and upbeat, and the spectators are usually well behaved. Fans around you will be only too happy to explain the rules.

The Workplace

If you are working in Australia you will, of course, have coworkers. It is common for Aussies to socialize over coffee, at lunch, and after work on a Friday in a favorite pub.

WHAT NEXT?

So, given these opportunities to meet Australians (and there are no doubt other opportunities), what do you do about it?

First, do not hesitate to introduce yourself. Aussies generally like the American approach of an outstretched hand and your name. In the work environment, or at a social function, or at a party in a friend's house, you are likely to be thought 'stand-offish' if you wait for an introduction.

Outside the work environment this is obviously more difficult, but it is seen as quite natural to speak to someone (one, not more—if there is a group it will be seen as intrusive) with whom you are sharing a table, or you are sitting next to at a bar or at a football game. Make a remark about the food, the view, or anything else that strikes you, and you will quickly discover if there is an opportunity for further conversation. Most people cannot resist a request for help, so asking for advice or directions will almost certainly get you a response.

Becoming a "Mate"

As outlined in Chapter 2, "mateship" was the kind of fellow-feeling that usually grew out of a shared experience of adversity, and could not be forced. In modern Australia there are not quite the same kinds of adversity to bring people together in mateship. As we have seen, wives or husbands, as well as bosses, the taxation office, and the police, could provide the adversity, and sticking by your friend through his or her troubles could be the foundation for a new kind of mateship.

But if, when you make friends, you learn about, or at least take an interest in, the interests of your new friends—whether it be live music, photography, cycling, rugby, Aboriginal art, gardening, or anything else—and share your interest with them, then you are on the right path. The next step is to join in—and actively share your common interest.

Shouting a Round

An old Australian saying had it that the worst thing you could do to a man was to steal his beer. Not his wife, or his tucker (food), or his horse, or his good name—but his *beer*.

There is a carry-over into today's culture, when Australians in a group at a bar take turns buying the next round of drinks. It is called "shouting." The term probably comes from

early times, when bars were very noisy places and you had to shout to get the barman's attention. To miss out on your shout—by going to the toilet, or suddenly remembering that you are supposed to be somewhere else, and leaving—means the end of your reputation.

Note for golfers: if you get a hole in one, then at the nineteenth hole—the club bar—you are obliged to shout a drink for everyone who is at the bar!

While something similar to "shouting" might apply in other countries, particularly in the UK, or sometimes in the USA, there are differences. Firstly it is never questioned in Australia. There is never any doubt about shouting, and whose shout it is. Secondly, shouting transcends rank, wealth, and gender. The boss joins in and takes her turn, as does the wealthiest person in the group, as does the one who may be "a bit strapped for cash" (one who doesn't have a lot of money.

As a visitor or new arrival, you will earn great respect if you step up early to the bar and say, "It's my shout," because you will be showing an understanding of and respect for a fine old—and continuing—Australian tradition. Keep acting that way, and you could easily find yourself in a situation of becoming a mate.

Receiving Invitations

Australians love to party. They might invite you to all kinds of events or functions—sporting, music, business, or family. They like to invite people to things they enjoy, and to share their enjoyment— it makes for more fun to have numbers involved. Going to a football game, out for dinner, to a pub or club for a few drinks, or cooking up a storm at home, are all much more enjoyable if they can invite someone or, better still, a number of people.

Your chances of being asked along to watch a sporting event depend very much on your having shown, in conversation, an appreciation and knowledge of that particular sport. If you happen to play it yourself, so much the better. Let them see you are an enthusiast. Australians love their sport, and they also love sharing it, either watching or playing, with other people of like mind.

Australians are good at return invitations, which will come as a result of your having invited *them* to something (see below). Don't forget that, when you are invited to an Australian home for a meal, you should take a decent bottle of wine along as a gift.

Some Australians like the idea of having their friends just dropping in for a drink, and this will often happen on a Saturday afternoon.

But not everyone welcomes this, so it would be sensible to check with friends rather than make a mistake. If you do drop in, take a bottle of their preferred "grog" (alcohol) along—and you'll be warmly welcomed!

And If You Don't Drink Alcohol?

If you don't drink alcohol, just politely refuse when it is offered. "Actually I don't drink," is fine, or "I'll just have a soft drink, thanks". Australians may be curious and might even ask you **_why_** you don't drink alcohol, but it will be quite generally accepted.

Entertaining

This should not be too much of a problem. Australians like to go out, and will be flattered that you ask them. Of course, your arrangements will vary according to your own circumstances. If you are living in a house or apartment it will be easy and natural to invite people to dinner or a barbecue there.

Otherwise, you can invite them to simply meet you in a bar, pub or club or to join you for breakfast, lunch or dinner—all of which are social opportunities these days, as people seem to eat out more. In this case it will not be expected that you will pay for everything. If it is your birthday, or a similar celebration, you might "shout" a few drinks (cocktails are very popular!). Should you decide to host a dinner party you should supply the drink, (beer, red and white wine, and perhaps a special cocktail such as a Caipirinha, Mojito, or Margarita). Rest assured that guests will pitch in and bring wine and/or beer. Your guests will be aware of the costs involved for you, and you can expect your invitation to be reciprocated by most of them.

For an informal meal or barbecue, beer and wine will usually be supplied, however it's a nice gesture to offer a nice bottle of wine —Australian, of course! You supply the food, and anything goes as Australians are getting increasingly sophisticated and creative with their barbecueing skills! Forget the stereotypical sausages and chops; expect—and learn to experiment with —chilli prawns, tandoori lamb, Brazilian style steaks, satay chicken, and chargrill vegetables. Invitations should be given at least one week in advance, or two weeks for a formal meal. Verbal invitations are fine.

chapter five

A GOD NAMED SPORT

Australians often appear to be very laid back, taking adversity and success in their stride. The two most famous Aussie catch phrases, "She'll be right" (everything will be fine), and "No worries" ("don't worry about it"), embrace the essence of the Spanish "*mañana*." But in one area they are very serious: sport.

This might be seen, mistakenly, as indicating that Australians don't work hard, or that they allow sport to interfere with work. Apart from being unwilling to attend Sunday breakfast meetings, there is another tradition: The first ten minutes of most Friday meetings will be given over to discussing the upcoming weekend's games—and the first ten minutes of Monday meetings will be devoted to a post-mortem / analysis / debrief of the weekend's sporting action, results, and—of course—all of those shocking / woeful ref's calls (referee's decisions). This is an equal opportunity activity, with women being as passionate and vocal as the men when it comes to "barracking" (supporting or shouting for) their local team. And, in Melbourne, where the following of the local game, Australian Rules football, is nothing less than fanatical, these discussions will be even longer and more heated / intense! There is a work ethic and there is a leisure ethic. The following is about the leisure ethic—mostly sports.

Australians draw a sharp distinction between work time and play time, and their favorite form of play is sport, whether as a spectator or a participant. Your surest way to acceptance is through being able to converse about sport, and of course it will help if you become involved in playing—there are always opportunities for running, cycling, swimming, paddle boarding, tennis, golf—or pretty much any sport you're interested in. It is not difficult to pick up local and international sports knowledge—hundreds of websites, acres of newsprint and hours of TV are devoted to it. An article about a key sportsman or sportswoman taking drugs, or having an affair with a teammate's wife or husband, will drive the war reports from the front page. Politicians scramble to be associated with sport—and current Prime Minister, Tony Abbott, well known for being a "MAMIL" (middle-aged man in lycra) is frequently seen participating in fun runs, charity cycle races, and—unfortunately—parading on the beach in his "budgie smugglers" (swimming trunks).

"Why are the Aussies so good at sport?" is an interesting question. At any Olympics, compared with the giant populations of the USA, Russia, and China, Australia, always "punches above its weight" considering its tiny population. Its record in world rugby, cricket, golf, tennis, swimming, sailing, and hockey, even soccer—the list goes on—is significant in any estimation.

THE CLIMATE AND THE GREAT OUTDOORS

At the level of "weekend" sport, some of the reasons for the general Aussie competence at sport are obvious. Climate and the relatively easy access to sporting facilities, and the great outdoors in general, plays a huge part in sporting life. Winters being generally short and mild, many ground sports can be played almost all year round. Many schools and homes, whether town or country, have swimming pools; and 80 percent of the population lives within around 30 miles (50 km) of the coast and the beaches. No wonder that many children are brought up swimming, surfing, playing tennis, or generally trying to get a ball into some sort of net or hoop. These leisure activities often turn to team sport as the children grow. Many parents find themselves acting as cab drivers on

Saturdays, driving the kids to their (usually very early morning) sports sessions to play for their school or local sports team.

Schools, local councils the RSL and other clubs all promote sport. There are sports facilities everywhere you look. Drive through the suburbs, or any country town, and you will see just how much of the land is given over to tennis courts, bowling lawns, cricket pitches, and all kinds of other sports grounds, centers, and facilities.

Aside from sport, Australians just like to be outdoors on weekends—going for a walk, or more strenuous bush walking; enjoying the beach; or simply lapping up the good weather sitting outside with a good coffee or a glass of something chilled!

THE OLYMPICS AND THE WORLD SCENE

This does not, however, really explain the success of Australians at Olympic and other international sports levels. Growing up with sport can be a precursor to success on the world scene, but few ever actually make it. In Australia more "make it", *per capita*, than in any other country in the world (if we discount those magnificent individual medal wins by lone athletes from tiny countries). A look at some

sporting history might cast some light on the
reasons, and will help you, the visitor, to relate
to Australia.

Cricket

Cricket is strongly associated with the British
(but is believed by some to have been invented
by the French). It was played in Australia in the
early 1800s. If you do not come from a cricket-
playing nation, I suggest that you read up about
what can be a most puzzling game (or what the
late comedian, Robin Williams, described as
"like baseball—played on valium").

The first Australian cricket team sent
to play in England, in the 1800s, was an all-
Aboriginal team. The Melbourne Cricket Club
was established in 1838, and the first Test match
between English and Australian cricketers was
played at the Melbourne Cricket Ground (the
MCG—now equally famous as the spiritual
home of Australian Rules Football), in 1876.
After that match there was talk of a Test Trophy
to commemorate England's loss. It was during
the next series in Australia that a ball, or the
stumps—the three wooden sticks hit into the
ground at each end of the pitch—were burnt
and the ashes saved in an urn, to be played for
as a trophy ever since. These are the "Ashes."

Acknowledged by even the British to be
the greatest cricketer of all time, the legendary

Sir Donald Bradman (1908–2001) remains one of the great Aussie icons.

But even the "gentleman's game" (the expression "not cricket" means not fair, or not honest), has not escaped controversy. To be a party to any discussion of cricket, at home or in the bar, you need to be aware of two infamous incidents. The first of these is the "bodyline" incident of 1932–3, when the England captain, Douglas Jardine instructed the bowler to bowl directly at Bradman's body in a manner likely to cause injury. Several Aussie batsmen were injured during this tour, and the anti-British feelings of the Australian public rose to fever pitch.

In the second incident, in 1981, Australia perpetrated the infamy. In a game against New Zealand, another traditional sporting foe, the NZ team, known as the Kiwis, needed six runs to win, with one ball to go—a difficult task, but not impossible. (A hit over the boundary earns six runs.) But it can only be done from traditional bowling, playing a fast ball. The Australian skipper, Greg Chappell, instructed the bowler, his brother Trevor, to bowl the last ball underarm, denying New Zealand the chance to hit a six. Shock! Horror! Australia's reputation for sportsmanship suffered, and underarm bowling was banned, being "underhand" and "not cricket."

Australian Rules Football, and Rugby
"Australian Rules" seems to the uninitiated to be a combination of rugby and soccer, but derives in fact from Gaelic football, as played in Ireland, but adjusted to Australian conditions. Aussie Rules, played in all states, is an authentic item of Australiana: its adherents, who have the fervor of the early Christians, would die in support of their team. They claim, with some validity, that this is the best spectator football game in the world.

In support of this, some years ago, when the two Melbourne teams with the most supporters, Collingwood and Carlton, were due to play the Grand Final at the MCG on the following Saturday, sixty thousand fans braved a wet winter's Thursday night just to watch the Collingwood team practice. In those days the MCG had grandstands and standing room and held some 118,000 spectators for the Grand Finals. Today the oval has seating room only, just over 100,000. An average of 60,000 spectators attend a game of the more popular AFL clubs.

The New South Wales supporters call their rugby "the game played in heaven." To Melbourne supporters of Aussie Rules, the MCG *is* "heaven."

Rugby is, of course, international; Aussie Rules is not. Two forms of rugby are played across Australia—Rugby Union (the old game, invented at Rugby School, England) and Rugby League (with changes in rules said to make it more exciting to watch). Rugby club games have traditionally not enjoyed the spectator support that Aussie Rules (AFL) does, yet the rise of the Super Rugby (Union) league (of fifteen Australian, New Zealand, and South African teams) is these days filling stadiums—just as Interstate and International games have always done.

Tennis and Golf

Australia has produced more than its share of tennis greats (though, sadly, there has been a bit of tennis 'drought' in terms of home grown grand slam winners in the past couple of decades). The Australian team claimed the Davis Cup, the most prestigious team-tennis event in the world, twenty times between

1939 and 2000. Some forty Wimbledon winners came from Australia, and the history of the sport could not be told without including the names of Lew Hoad, Ken Rosewall, Rod Laver, Margaret Court, John Newcombe, Evonne Goolagong-Cawley, Pat Cash, Pat Rafter, and Lleyton Hewitt, and more recently Bernard Tomic and Nick Kyrgios.

Golf is not the preserve of a moneyed elite, as it is in so many parts of the world, but can be enjoyed by all. As well as some fine private golf courses open to members' guests, there are many public courses. Greg Norman (the Great White Shark) is perhaps still Australia's best-known male golfer, as world champion for a number of years, though Adam Scott and Stuart Appleby have enjoyed recent success, and Carrie Webb the best-known female, has also been a world champion.

Skiing

The existence of extensive world-class ski-fields comes as a surprise to some visitors. Many Australians and visitors ski in the ski-fields in the highlands between Sydney and Melbourne. The season is generally June to September. Check with a travel agent for transport, accommodation, ski rental, and ski lift passes.

Boats

This is another Australian passion. There are big and small boats—and big and small yachtsmen (kids can be seen skidding around Sydney Harbour and other waterways in tiny single or multihull yachts). It is estimated that there are some 180,000 yachtsmen and women,

over 100,000 speedboat owners in Australia. Australia has competed in the prestigious sailing event The America's Cup (named not after the country but the first winner, the yacht *America*) since 1962. In 1983 Australia, with

---

THE MELBOURNE CUP

Australia comes to a stop shortly before 3.00 p.m. on the first Tuesday of every November. A hush settles over the land from the Northern Territory to Tasmania, while one of the great horse races of the world is run. The first Melbourne Cup was run in 1861, over a distance of 2 miles. When the metric system was adopted, in 1972, it was shortened to 3.2 kilometers.

The preferred method of betting on the Cup (millions of people who would otherwise never place a bet do so on this race) is in the office "sweep," or pool. You will certainly be invited to participate. Everybody puts in, say, $5, and the names of all the horses are drawn randomly from a hat against the names of each member of staff. This eliminates the need to know anything about horse racing—but requires that time be taken off to watch the race. Work stops, across the nation. The entire pot (all the money) is divided appropriately amongst the winner and the two runners-up.

the yacht *Australia II*, became the first nation
to take the cup away from America since the
inaugural race in 1851.

A LAND OF OPPORTUNITY

So Australians live in a land of sporting
opportunity, with the climate, the proximity
of the beaches, and the wide-open spaces, all
contributing to sporting endeavor. They often
take up sports while very young, playing one
form in winter and often more than one in
summer, at school, then for the District or
Club, for the State, and then, of course, some
for their country. Why do they do so well
internationally?

Anyone who has achieved success at a
national level and beyond will tell you that
it takes more than natural ability, early
experience, training, and practice. To start
training before dawn and finish in the dark all
year round; to diet and exercise continually;
to forgo most social life; to struggle to improve
one's performance, and to hurt, strain, and
torture tired muscles—all these and more
require something else.

The Aboriginal peoples have supplied
some of Australia's best sportsmen and women.
Also, from the time of their arrival, the new
Australian settlers set out with something to
prove. They had to conquer a harsh land and

overcome the disadvantages of arriving with little, in many cases nothing. They were looked down on as convicts, or at best as colonials. They needed to succeed.

All this applied in sport as well as in life; in fact, in the beginning, there was only work and sport. Some were driven more than others— and were more successful than others—but they set the benchmark and then raised it higher

and higher, pulling the rest up with them. There can be no doubt that high standards, and the adulation of their young compatriots to those who set them, have contributed to an intense

desire to emulate these sporting heroes.

Massive media coverage of these men and women and their achievements provides an irresistible challenge to many young people. Success breeds success. As a result, many Australian adults play and enjoy a social game; many participate in competitive matches; some give their all in major events; and the heroes are international conquerors.

Not all Australians are active sportsmen and women. As a visitor you will not automatically be expected to have sporting accomplishments: it is understood not to be within everybody's ability—or areas of interest. You will find many Australians who are passionate and knowledgeable about the arts —literature, art, opera, and theater. However, the majority of Australians enjoy sports at some level. You will be comfortably accepted into Australian society at any level if you can join in discussions on sport and sporting achievements both in Australia and in your own country. If you talk about your country's successes, expect some good-natured banter. Any suggestion that another country is good at sport will be irresistible to the Aussie sense of humor. But you can also expect respect for your interest and knowledge.

culture smart! australia

TIME OUT

FOOD AND DRINK

Thanks to the Greek god Dionysus, and the Roman Bacchus, for the changes the Greeks and Italians made to Anglo influenced Australian cuisine (at that time really an oxymoron) from the 1950s. Thanks to all the later immigrants who brought with them their wonderful varieties of food and cooking styles, and to the six generations of wine makers that have established a place for Australian red and white wines internationally and on the wine lists of some of the most sophisticated restaurants in Paris, New York, and Beijing.

And thanks to the Lebanese, Vietnamese, Indonesians, Indians, French, Thais, Chinese, Africans, Japanese, Brazilians, and Chileans for contributing to what has become one of the most varied international culinary scenes. Indeed, apart from the plethora of specialty ethnic restaurants to be found in the major cities, Australian "foodies" excel in blending their excellent home produced fish, meat, vegetables and fruit with Asian, South American, or North African influences to produce "fusion" food—definitely the best of all culinary worlds!

Fresh Food

Australia's great varieties of climate, from the tropics in the north, through irrigated plains and mountains, to coasts with Mediterranean climates, mean that a multitude of fresh ingredients are readily available—from paw-paw (papaya), bananas, pineapples, avocados, and mangoes in the north to nectarines, peaches, apricots, strawberries, raspberries, and apples in the south. Immigrants have given Australia lemongrass, eggplant (aubergine), zucchini, garlic, basil, coriander, artichoke, bok choy, shiitake mushroom, and on and on and on—all fresh daily in your local supermarket or vegetable market.

Australian beef is good enough to be exported to the USA. The lamb is nearly as good as New Zealand lamb. The pork is rich (and a little fatty, which gives it taste, unlike much European pork).

And the fish! Because of the length of Australia's coastline, from warm tropical waters off the Queensland coast to cold waters off southern Australia, you can sample barramundi, mud crabs, and coral trout from the north; prawns and world-famous oysters from New South Wales, Tasmania, and South Australia; deep-sea whiting, crayfish, lobster, and cultivated Atlantic salmon in the south.

Some Australian old time-favorites

Anzac biscuits
Biscuits made from rolled oats and honey. As sent to the Anzac troops at Gallipoli during World War I.

Balmain bugs (and Moreton Bay Bugs)
A type of small, saltwater crayfish.

Chiko rolls
Deep-fried rolls filled with savory vegetables.

Damper
A flat bread made with flour and water and baked in the embers of a fire.

Finger buns
Long, narrow yeast buns covered with pink icing.

Floater
A meat pie floating in mashed potato, gravy, and mushy green peas.

Lamington
A sponge cake square, covered with a thin layer of chocolate and desiccated coconut.

Pavlova
A meringue base piled high with fruit and cream, named after the lightness of the famous ballerina.

Sausage rolls
Sausage meat wrapped in pastry.

Vegemite
Australia's most famous and much loved spread, made from yeast extract.

Violet Crumble Bar
Made by Hoadleys, a revered confection made from honeycomb covered with chocolate.

Yabbies
Small, freshwater crayfish.

Wines

Australians enjoy a drink, but their palates and choices are becoming more sophisticated. Although beer is still the most widely consumed beverage by volume, Australia is these days also a wine-drinking nation. Australia not only produces some of the best wine in the world, but it drinks home-grown as well, with 85 percent of Australia's wine consumption being a robust Aussie red or a cheeky sav blanc. While Australia represents just 4 percent of global production, it is now the sixth largest producer and one of the top four exporters of wine in the world. Australia sells more wine in the UK than in any other country, satisfies China's new thirst for red wine, and in a 'coals to Newcastle' credibility coup actually sells wine to France! Australia's wine industry has suffered In recent years along with its overseas competitors, as global wine production has expanded faster than demand—resulting in a decline in world wine prices and declining profit margins for Australia's winemakers.

While not good for the industry, it means that your "favorite drop" may be very reasonably priced if you buy carefully (see next page for advice). And there's always BYO!

For any wine-loving visitor, an hour's drive from most capital cities will have you sitting in a cellar-door tasting room, sipping some of the world's finest wine. Many of these vineyards are in beautiful countryside, have top notch restaurants, and can be visited as part of a conducted wine tour. It's well worth signing up for a bus tour of one of the wine regions, as it affords you special access to organised group tasting sessions, and, apart from anything else, avoids you running foul of Australia's strictly enforced drinking and driving regulations (a blood alcohol level of over .05 percent could lead to a fine and loss of driver's license).

The advantage of a tour is that most of the approximately 1,500 vineyards are clustered in distinct regions, and it is relatively easy to make visits to different vineyards and be back in the city for dinner. Examples of these are the Mornington Peninsula, south of Melbourne; the Adelaide Hills, McLaren Vale or the Barossa Valley outside of Adelaide; the Hunter Valley (90 minutes north of Sydney) and Margaret River, south of Perth. You can get further information and descriptions

BYO—BRING YOUR OWN

This concept, which is very common in Australia, means that you can take your own wine to many restaurants. Imagine the savings! Buy your wine at a good price in one of the many bottle shops you will find dotted around cities and suburbs (somewhat similar to USA liquor stores and UK off licenses, they offer a very wide choice of wines)—and take it to the restaurant you fancy.

You should note that most restaurants that accept BYO will state the fact in the window, on the menu, and in their advertisements. Others that have liquor licenses will allow you to bring your wine and will supply glasses, but will charge you corkage—perhaps a couple of dollars for each drinker. Even so, you will save considerably by buying at a bottle shop. More sophisticated, expensive restaurants are fully licensed and do not allow BYO. So make sure to enquire before making a reservation. Then you can decide whether or not you wish to pay the extra for what might well be superior food and drink. You can also avoid the embarrassment of finding that the restaurant *is* BYO, that all your friends have turned up toting bottles of wine, and that you have turned up empty-handed!

of individual wineries from the websites of state tourist offices.

Almost half of Australia's total grape harvest is produced in the state of South Australia, with about half of the state's wine production coming from the Riverland, a region irrigated by two of Australia's largest rivers, the Murray and the Darling, which merge near the borders of New South Wales, Victoria, and South Australia. Further breaking down total wine production by State, about a third is produced in New South Wales, about 15 percent comes from Victoria, with the rest being produced by the cooler soils of Tasmania and the higher altitudes and rich volcanic soils of Queensland's inland ranges. Social convention dictates that bottles of wine are opened for visitors and at dinner parties—and you are judged by your choice of wine. Remember, too, that it is polite to open wine brought by a guest —unless the hosts have carefully selected wines to pair with their dinner menu.

Buying Wines
- Price is a guide to quality, but it is also advisable to read the wine reviews online or in newspapers for tips on the good wines currently available. Buy from major liquor outlets rather than from pubs/hotels.
- Perfectly acceptable wine to take to friends can be bought for under $20–25 a bottle.
- Good wines probably cost over $30 a bottle, exceptional wines over $60.

- As the roughest of guides to grape and district, try the following. (Australian labels are tightly controlled by the Trade Practices Act, accurately describing origin, contents, year, and alcoholic content; and you can read the label.)

Red Wines
- Shiraz (claret from the Rhône) from McLaren Vale, Barossa Valley, or Central Victoria.
- Cabernet Sauvignon (the great grape of Bordeaux) from Coonawarra, Barossa Valley, or Margaret River.
- Cabernet/Shiraz from any of the above areas.
- Merlot from BarossaValley, McLaren Vale, or Central Victoria.
- Pinot Noir (original grape from Burgundy) from Tasmania, Yarra Valley, or Mornington Peninsula.

White Wines
- Chardonnay from anywhere—said to be "a promiscuous grape—grows anywhere."
- Riesling (originally Rhine Riesling) from the Clare Valley, Coonawarra, Tasmania.
- Semillon (a Bordeaux grape) from the Hunter Valley (must be a few years old); or South Australia or Goulburn Valley (to drink now).

If you have a real interest in wines, and you have not been to New Zealand, try some of their white wines from Cloudy Bay or the Marlborough region, readily available in Australia.

RESTAURANTS

As has been said, Australia offers perhaps the greatest variety of ethnic cuisines anywhere in the world, from Moroccan to Chinese in its many forms—the ubiquitous Chinese restaurants are today the purveyors of Cantonese, Pekingese, Szechuan (Szechwan), Hakka, and Shanghai food, cooked by people from the place of origin. Many city and suburban shopping centers, and other locations such as Chinatown and Darling Harbour in Sydney, have this wide variety, offered from many small outlets, side by side. "Take out Thai'" is competing on the high street as the post-pub "filler", replacing Greek kebabs, which, in turn, had replaced fish and chips a few decades ago as the traditional late night takeaway of choice.

Special Occasion?

If you decide to eat out in an expensive or very popular restaurant, it might be best to go on a Wednesday, Thursday, or Friday night—in that order of preference. A Saturday night is likely to be busier, noisier, and more difficult to get a table reservation.

TABLE MANNERS

Table manners generally follow the British tradition. If the food does not need to be cut with a knife, it is quite correct just to use a fork in the

right hand; but otherwise Australians do not cut
up their food and then put the knife down and eat
with a fork in the American way. The knife should
be held (with the handle covered by your hand, not
like a pencil), while the fork (facing down) lifts the
food. It is polite to put them both down on the plate
while you chew your mouthful or converse with
your table companions.

At the end of the course the knife and fork are
placed together in the center of the plate, with
the fork facing upward, so that the waiter or your
hostess will know that you have finished eating;
but the table will be cleared only when everyone
has finished. Knife and fork laid separately on a
plate on which there is still some food indicates
to the waiter that you have not finished.

The bill for a group of people is usually divided
and shared, singles (men and women) paying their
single share and the couple paying double.

As a visitor—particularly to Australia's "red
center"—you may well be encouraged by a tour
guide to try some kind of "bush tucker." Interest
in this has grown recently, since new Australians
have come to appreciate that Aborigines survived
healthily on local food for centuries before white
man's food was introduced—in the very early
days this was all imported.

You might be offered witchetty grubs, either
cooked or raw and live. These are the larvae of
wood-boring moths found in holes in tree trunks,
and visitors find them fascinating in a way that

is certainly not shared by most locals. If you do accept an offer to try this delicacy (or another, the honey ant—a fat ant which stores a honeylike substance in its abdomen), remember to hold them by the head and eat the rest, or bite the head off first.

Kangaroo, camel, crocodile, emu and other delicacies have also found their way on to some restaurant menus as chefs

experiment with the lean protein and robust flavors offered by Australia's home-grown form of "game."

It is worth noting that unlike restaurants in the US, the word "entrée" means (as it should) the starter, or first course.

THE "BARBIE," OR "BAR-B-QUE"

Not much needs to be said about a "barbie." The old typical party scenario, in which the guys stayed around the beer keg or esky (cold bottle carrier) while the women made the salads and prepared the nibbles in the kitchen is thankfully long gone. These days, the barbecue fare is more creative and the planning and cooking process is very much an equal opportunity activity! However, in some domains, old habits

TIPPING

Perhaps because of the egalitarian spirit in Australia, tipping is not the problem it can be in other countries. Australians tend to feel that a waiter or waitress should earn a tip through extra or very friendly service. Given that, they are recognized as not being well paid and most Australians will "share the wealth" (pass on some of their money to help another) by paying a little more than the bill requires. Typically private customers tip about 10 percent, and businessmen 15 percent. The GST (Goods and Services Tax) will be shown on the bill. In more casual coffee shops and restaurants patrons may just "round up" the bill and leave a few gold coins ($1 and $2) rather than rigidly sticking to the 10 percent calculation.

and traditional roles die hard—and on arrival the men may huddle around the grill to flex their barbecue muscle and weigh in on the best cooking technique—to turn or not to turn? Frequently, there will be one designated cook who's allowed to brandish the barbecue tongs—surrounded by ten expert consultants whose advice —liberally laced with good-natured sarcasm and insults— will come thick and fast and not infrequently in direct proportion to the amount of beer and wine consumed.

If invited to a barbecue, it is customary to ask if you can bring something. In fact (except among close friends—who might all pitch in with appetizers, salads, and desserts) this offer is usually refused. But do take a good bottle of wine.

TAKEAWAYS

One of the less fortunate types of food import has been American-style fast food. Overeating of Kentucky Fried Chicken, McDonald's burgers and French fries, and the like, has brought about a weight revolution, and many Australians have joined their American cousins in their obesity problem. Some 60 percent of Australian adults and 25 percent of children are now classified as technically overweight or obese—an increase of 5 percent over the past twenty years. In recent years, however, there has been a backlash, driven mainly by general concern about children growing up unfit and with a "junk-food mentality." As a result, Australians are now much more health-food conscious—learning to eschew sugar-laden processed foods and drinks.

For you, the tourist, the deep-fried foods are there—everywhere—if you want them. And you might just try some of the best fish and chips to be had, battered and salted, along with fried calamari and potato scallops (like a hash brown). However, wander into the local fish and chip shop, and you'll find a wonderful array of fresh fish that's grilled or barbecued that can come with salad, instead of chips. Similarly, every Australian high street has a 'chicken shop' selling roast chicken with a healthy choice of roast vegetables and—a much healthier option than the Colonel's deep fried alternative.

AUSTRALIAN CULTURE
Customs and Traditions

If you know little else about Australian customs when you arrive in the country, you will need to know about the tradition of Anzac Day. Wherever you find yourself on April 25—considered by most Australians as their most important holiday—there will be an Anzac Day parade. On this day old and young soldiers march together to the local war memorial, to the accompaniment of a brass band. Children join in the parade alongside their soldier fathers and grandfathers. At the war memorial there will be speeches, a minute's silence, and the reverent intonation of Laurence Binyon's "Poem for the Fallen":

> *They shall not grow old,*
> * as we that are left grow old.*
> *Age shall not weary them,*
> * nor the years condemn.*
> *At the going down of the sun*
> * and in the morning,*
> *We will remember them.*

In every RSL (Returned Soldiers League) club across the land, at 6:00 p.m., the poker machines will cease their cacophony and a hush will settle over the people, who turn to face west and offer a minute's silence for those who fell in battle.

Why?

Anzac Day commemorates the enormous sacrifices made by the Anzacs (the Australian and New Zealand Army Corps) in the First World War, in the Allied attempt at Gallipoli, in Turkey, to force a way through the Dardanelles and link up with Russia. History confirms that this attempt was doomed from the start. Much of the tragedy lies in the fact that the military commanders, from Winston Churchill down, made a terrible blunder. Thousands of troops were landed on the beach at Gallipoli, to be shot down by fire from established Turkish machine gun posts, their bodies piling up to be climbed over by the next wave.

Between April 25 and December 19, 1915, over eight thousand Australians and two thousand New Zealanders were killed (two thousand on the first day alone), and nineteen thousand Australians wounded, in a battle on the other side of the world, defending the British Empire.

The bravery of these men in the face of hopeless odds, the nobility of their courage in attempting the impossible, and their legendary mateship unto death, won them a reputation that endures to this day. The Australian film director Peter Weir's outstanding movie *Gallipoli,* made in 1981, conveys this well. It is well worth seeing— both as a great piece of film making, and as an iconic story in Australia's history.

The Gay and Lesbian Mardi Gras
Sydney has been called the "gay capital" of the Southern Hemisphere—and this is certainly true during Mardi Gras, when a carnival atmosphere descends on Oxford Street, and 5,000 flamboyantly dressed men and women and dozens of floats parade along one of the city's main thoroughfares   Half a million people—in some cases, whole families—wave and cheer from the sidelines. In an expression of what is, to many older Australians (who were brought up in an era when "queer" bashing, for some, was rife) great tolerance; even the gay men and women of the New South Wales police force has a float!

Ballet, Opera, Music, Literature
Australians have excelled in ballet and dance, despite the country's macho self-image. There are several thousand ballet schools across the country, arising from the examples, traditions, and innovations of distinguished world-renown

dancers such as Sir Robert Helpmann in the 1920s and 1930s; Marilyn Jones in the 1960s; and, more recently, Lisa Bolte, Meryl Tankard, and Graham Murphy.

Australia has produced a number of world-class operatic singers, such as Dame Nellie Melba, in the nineteenth century, Dame Joan Sutherland, John Brownlee, and Peter Dawson in the twentieth. The prestigious Australian Opera was established in the early 1970s.

An important figure in Australian musical development was Sir Bernard Heinze, who in the late 1920s became musical advisor to the Australian Broadcasting Commission. With his knowledge and inspiration he helped to bring a range of high-quality orchestral music to the Australian public. Other famous musical names include the composer Percy Grainger, the concert pianist Eileen Joyce, and the classical guitarist John Williams.

On a lighter and more contemporary musical note, Iggy Azalea, Sia, Keith Urban, Jet, and Wolfmother, continue the legacy of Silverchair, Powderfinger, and Savage Garden and, if your memory goes back this far—continue the legacy of the Bee Gees, Crowded House, INXS, Men At Work, Midnight Oil, Little River Band, AC/DC, and the Black Sorrows by making their mark on the world's music scene. Two essentially Australian bands are Gondwanaland, blending white and Aboriginal music, and the Aboriginal Yothu Yindi, with a great mix of traditional sound and modern technology. Meanwhile musician Geoffrey Gurrumul Yunupingu has been described by *Rolling Stone* magazine as "Australia's most

important voice"; along with fellow Aboriginal singer, Jessica Mauboy, Gurrumul has performed to President Obama at the White House. Then there are the singers and actors Olivia Newton-John and Kylie Minogue, Natalie Imbruglia,

and Delta Goodrem. The Australian TV soap opera *Neighbours* and *Home and Away* are viewed around the world, and have provided a platform for the launch of many young actors' careers, including Russell Crowe, Naomi Watts, Chris Hemsworth, Guy Pearce, Heath Ledger, Dannii Minogue, Ryan Kwanten, and Simon Baker.

The Australian literary scene will provide the visitor with distinctly Australian voices on singularly Australian themes. Read the following, and you will be better equipped than many of your hosts:

Capricornia and, if you have the time,
  Poor Fellow My Country by Xavier Herbert.
The Eye of the Storm, and others by
  Patrick White.
The Chant of Jimmy Blacksmith, and others
  by Thomas Keneally.
Cloudstreet by Tim Winton.
An Imaginary Life by David Malouf.
True History of the Kelly Gang by Peter Carey.
The Tyranny of Distance by Geoffrey Blainey.
The Fatal Shore by Robert Hughes.
Unreliable Memoirs by Clive James.
The Thorn Birds by Colleen McCulloch.
A Town Like Alice by Nevil Shute.

Other Australian writers of note include Miles Franklin, Germaine Greer, Christina Stead, Helen Garner, Bryce Courtney, Elizabeth Jolley, and and see the works listed under "Further Reading" at the end of this book.

Painting

Aboriginal art, traditionally executed on cave walls, strips of bark, wood, and their own bodies, chiefly using ochre, has achieved an international reputation in recent decades. Rock art is concentrated in northern areas of Australia, with the largest collection located in Kakadu National Park and neighboring Arnhem Land— it is the most extraordinary collection in the world. Especially well known are the dot-mosaic and X-ray styles of painting, depicting animals with their skeletal structure and internal organs. Examples can be seen in all major public galleries, and can be readily purchased in galleries and Aboriginal shops. Artists like Albert Namatjira transferred their talents to watercolors and oils.

The works of white artists grew away from the early colonials' depictions of Australian scenes.

The painters S. T. Gill, Tom Roberts, Arthur Streeton, Fred Williams, and Fred McCubbin are widely credited with viewing and representing the Australian landscape through Australian, not European eyes.

Styles changed little until the social-realist depictions of immigrants and the working classes by Noel Counihan and Josi Bergner. Sidney Nolan contributed near abstracts of the bushranger (robber) Ned Kelly, and some depictions of famous historical events; William Dobell, portraiture; and Russell Drysdale, stark outback landscapes and lifestyles.

Australian art today is diverse, and is perhaps more modern in its appreciation of the natural environment. Designer Ken Done's has added graphic art work—mainly vividly colorful abstracts of Sydney harbor— which was so prolific in the 1980s that Australians referred to his body of work as "over-Done"—however he continues to be successful with his endless variations on the same irresistible theme, and Brett Whitley's canvases are vibrant explorations of landscapes and domestic situations.

Cinema

Australians made movies before the 1950s. Some were pretty awful—and they still turn out some dross at times. But there are also some giants of the Australian industry: cinematographers like

Peter Weir—*Picnic at Hanging Rock* (1975), *Gallipoli* (1981), *Fearless* (1993), *Dead Poet's Society* (1989); Fred Schepesi—*The Chant of Jimmy Blacksmith* (1978); *Six Degrees of Separation* (1993); Bruce Beresford—*The Getting of Wisdom* (1977), *Breaker Morant* (1980), *Driving Miss Daisy* (1990); Gillian Armstrong—*My Brilliant Career* (1978), *Little Women* (1995). Other movies of note include *Strictly Ballroom*, *Mad Max*, *Crocodile Dundee*, *Priscilla Queen of the Desert*, and *Lantana*.

Some Australian actors who have gained an international reputation are Nicole Kidman, Toni Collette, Cate Blanchett, Rose Byrne, Naomi Watts, Judy Davis, Mel Gibson, Brian Brown, Geoffrey Rush, Simon Baker, Rachel Griffiths, Sam Neill, Jack Thomson, Hugo Weaving, Guy Pearce, the late Heath Ledger, Russell Crowe, Chris Hemsworth, and Sam Worthington.

Contemporary Australians are creating a new and vibrant cultural tradition.

chapter **seven**

TRAVEL, HEALTH, & SAFETY

GOING WALKABOUT

It will be obvious to a visitor that there is a lot to
see and do in Australia. While most people tend to
over plan overseas trips, this is one country where
forward planning will greatly improve your stay.
Many visitors want to see the Great Barrier Reef,
Uluru (Ayers Rock), and Bondi Beach in Sydney,
and to have a meal in one of the fine restaurants
of Melbourne.

But Townsville, in Queensland, from where
you can take a plane or boat to the reef just
halfway up the reef's length, is about 850 miles

(1,367 km) from Brisbane, which in turn is nearly the same distance from Sydney. Melbourne is about 540 miles (873 km) from Sydney. Uluru via Alice Springs is over 1,200 miles (nearly 2,000 km) if you are flying from Sydney, but many more (1,820 miles, or 2,931 km) if you are traveling by road.

Wherever you land, which will most likely be in Sydney, Melbourne, or Perth, it is a good idea to give yourself a few days to adjust your body clock—both from jetlag and from differences in seasons, especially if you have arrived from the Northern Hemisphere—before you set out to tackle these vast distances.

The following pages will help you to make your travel plans, to make decisions about destinations, and to select from the almost overwhelming number of choices. They will also help you to understand some of the differences between the Australian states, and the differing attitudes of the Australians who live in them.

PLANNING YOUR TRIP

Going on holiday can be one of the most memorable events of your life. But it can be memorably *good* or memorably *bad*. The fact is that it can become a nightmare if you rely totally on travel agents or tour operators.

These day you are able to research every aspect of your trip including making bookings for flights,

Some Travel Tips

Australia is a very user-friendly country when it comes to travel, but you need to be careful about some things:

Free extras

Nothing is free—you will be paying somewhere.

Package deals

Many claim to be cheap and to save you money. You will get what you have paid for—a low standard.

Hidden extras

Look for things like charges for washing bed linens; key deposits; taxes.

Hostel chains

Some are excellent; many are not.

Discount cards

These generally offer no better deal than you can negotiate yourself.

Credit card numbers

Give these only as a last resort to secure a booking.

Valuables

Store these with Reception, and obtain a receipt.

car hire, accommodation, concerts, festivals and tours, so your decisions are well informed.

If you deal with a travel agent, be sure to tell them exactly what you want. If they recommend certain airlines, accommodation, etc., check prices and alternatives elsewhere. The agent may be working on commission for clients. So shop around before you buy, because prices can vary considerably. Don't make quick decisions—it's a long way to travel to get it wrong! Double check travel agent or online booking services' refund

policy, and make sure you have travel insurance—
particularly if you're planning on engaging in some
of the fabulous extreme sports and other outdoor
activities that Australia offers.

STATE DIFFERENCES AND RIVALRIES

The rivalry between states is largely, but not
entirely, in fun, and should be understood by
visitors in that light. An example derives from
the fact that the New South Wales police have,
over the years, suffered allegations of corruption,
and some of these have been corroborated
by investigations through a number of Royal
Commissions. Visitors should note that the
corruption has been internal, and at a high level—
heaven help anyone who thinks he can bribe an
ordinary policeman during the performance of
his duties. Equally, the Victorian police have a
reputation for shooting (criminals) first and asking
questions later. A favorite story shared by people in
both states concerns a big cross-border raid made
by police from both states in the 1990s. The NSW
police are claimed to have said to the Victorian
police, "Look, we won't take anything if you don't
shoot anybody."

Sydney, New South Wales, with a population of
close to five million, is the largest city in Australia.
It has taken over from its closest rival, Melbourne,
as the financial center of the country, and likes to
think of itself as the more worldly capital. After all,

it has the Gay and Lesbian Mardi Gras, topless beaches, rugby, and the Opera House (as the locals will tell you, often in that order).

Manly and Bondi Beaches are popular favorites with tourists, and Sydneysiders know that they have the best beaches, the best harbor, and the best climate. Of Melbourne, they will say things like: "It's a terrible place. I went there once and it was raining," or, "the best thing to come out of Melbourne is the Hume Highway" (it goes to Sydney). Sydneysiders look down on all other state capitals, but particularly Melbourne.

Melbourne, Victoria, has a population of more than four million. It was the financial center of Australia, and is considered the cultural center, and more "Victorian" (as in Victorian 1890s England) in attitude and style than Sydney. The "Vics" (Victorians) will cheerfully tell you that this is because Melbourne was settled by free settlers, while Sydney was settled by convicts—"and it still shows."

Melbourne is said to be the second-largest Greek city in the world, after Athens. Also, more immigrant Italians stayed in Melbourne than in any other city. This, together with the arrival of other immigrants from elsewhere, has given the city a cosmopolitan variety of restaurants—arguably more so than Sydney.

A good Melbourne story relates a comment made by the American actress Ava Gardner, when she was starring in the movie *On the Beach* in 1959. She was asked what she thought of Melbourne. She said: "Well, the movie is about the end of the world—and they couldn't have found a better place." Today, Melbourne is a far cry from that desolate image; it is an elegant modern city with some beautiful buildings on wide, tree-lined streets with open-air dining. Melburnians are justly proud of their art galleries and theaters.

As a visitor you will be made very welcome—particularly if you don't tell them that you visited Sydney first. Melburnians look down on all other state capitals and try to ignore Sydney.

Brisbane, Queensland, has a population of 2.2 million. Queenslanders have a saying about their state and the climate: "beautiful one day, perfect the next." This will be said to you with a straight face (and as a visitor, the best advice is for you to keep a straight face too)—a face from which they are wiping the beads of perspiration resulting from high humidity and high temperatures. They are inordinately proud of their Gold Coast. The Sunshine coast, where you will find the town of Noosa, is lush and tropical. Further north, in fact as far as Port Douglas, the coast has some beautiful beaches, and interesting country towns providing ready access to the Great Barrier Reef.

Queenslanders look down on people from "south of the border" (with New South Wales), calling them "Mexicans" (truly). As a visitor, you can claim you were just "passing through" New South Wales in order to get to Queensland.

Darwin, on the coast of the Northern Territory, has a population of over 110,000. The remote splendor of the environment, the relaxed lifestyle, the multicultural mix, and a younger than average population give it a distinctively frontier feel.

Adelaide, South Australia, referred to as "the city of churches," has a population of over one million. A Colonel Light, who laid it out neatly on a "square" of nearly equal sides, designed the city. The settlers were all free, many coming on paid voyages directly to South Australia, and the place has a reputation for being rather staid and quiet: "well laid out and ready to be buried," according to Sydneysiders and Melburnians. The city is charming, with fine restaurants in tree-lined streets, and a calming pace of life. A travel writer once wrote, "Adelaide is a delightful place to stop—for lunch."

Adelaidians also have a reputation for being snobbish. It is said that, on being introduced to you, they ask not where you come from, what your job is, or how much you earn, but what school you went to. (But although they may look down on folk from all the other states because they didn't go to the "right" school, many of them leave to go to university in other states.)

However, the city belies its staid and stuffy reputation. It has many more hotels per head of population than other capitals; it had topless bars before the other states; and it had an allegedly gay Premier who was supported by the people, who advanced civil rights, and who gave great support to an event of international importance—the Adelaide Festival of the Arts. Nearby is the Barossa Valley, home of some fine Australian wineries, and a delightful area to visit (and sample).

Perth, Western Australia, has a population of over one million. It is the most isolated modern city in the world. This has an effect on the collective psyche of its inhabitants—they are aware that they are isolated, and they are glad of it. Western Australians ironically call Australians from the eastern seaboard (especially Sydney and Melbourne) "the Wise Men from the East"—a biblical metaphor. Western Australians resent the way Sydneysiders and Melburnians tell them how to run their state. Western Australia, having most of the gold and nickel, and reserves of oil and timber, is, they say, the only financially independent state.

Perth has a warm climate, miles of enticing beaches, and all that money. Perth people are very friendly to anybody who is not from Sydney or Melbourne (South Australians are just acceptable, being also somewhat distant from the "Wise Men"—and it is doubtful if Western Australians can relate at all to Tasmanians or Queenslanders, who are further away, geographically, than Singaporeans). As a visitor from overseas, however, you will be most welcome.

Canberra, Australian Capital Territory, the Federal Capital and Seat of Government, has a population of more than three hundred thousand. Australians visiting from other cities deny this, claiming that there are actually no people there, just controlled robot figures that drive robot cars at regular intervals around empty buildings. When you visit the city, you will see what they mean. However, Canberra does have a wonderful gardener—it is a very pretty city, especially during the spring flower festival, Floriade. The National Gallery of Australia in Canberra is the best gallery in the country, housing Aboriginal and other Australian art, along with a fine international collection; there is a huge War Memorial, and a distinguished Parliament House. And it is close to Sydney.

Hobart, Tasmania, has a population of over 200,000. The Tasmanians are most welcoming folk, with strong ties to the UK, and Tasmania is a wonderful place for a relaxing holiday. It also offers the best opportunity you will have to see what the convict days were really like—at Port Arthur. Mainlanders will tell you that the Tasmanians welcome any visitors—for someone to talk to.

The Tasmanians in general do not look much further than their coast, and Tasmania is likewise sometimes forgotten by the rest of Australia. Once, at the Commonwealth Games held in Brisbane, there was an opening display by schoolchildren, who gathered in the arena to form a map of Australia—but they forgot to include Tasmania.

TRANSPORT
Buses
The great majority of Australians live in cities where urban transport is much the same as any other metropolitan areas around the world.

City and suburban buses carry commuters and visitors, as do trains, trams (streetcars, which operate in Melbourne and Adelaide), and tour buses. The main tour bus company in Australia is McCaffertys/Greyhound, which maintains a country-wide service. There are several other companies, operating mostly between Sydney, Melbourne, and Adelaide. The best way to travel around Australia by bus is with a Bus Pass. These

can be based on distance, or have a number of months' validity. Buying sector fares is more expensive than the Pass, and should be considered only if you going from A to B in less than a week. There are some great tour buses, such as Wayward Bus and Oz Experience, but they travel only between large backpacker resorts.

Trains

Australia has some of the world's great train journeys. Check out the Indian Pacific (from Sydney via Adelaide to Perth), the Ghan, named after Afghan camel trains (from Adelaide to Alice Springs and soon through to Darwin), and the Queenslander (from Brisbane to Cairns).

The Indian Pacific covers the longest stretch of straight rail in the world (over 300 miles, or 500 km, without a bend), and the Ghan covers the longest north–south rail line in the world.

There is no Australian equivalent of the Euro Pass, However, there are many good deals to be had in nearly all states on passes as well as discount specials. Remember that Australia is a huge country, and some of these trips are measured in days rather than hours.

For state-run trains, call the transport information number in the state capital, or any travel agent.

Flying

Qantas and Virgin Blue are the two main airlines within Australia, and both offer special fares for domestic (internal) and international travel. Booking is available, and is often cheaper, on the Internet. Within each state there are regional airlines, which can also offer good deals.

It is a good idea to check with your local travel agent about special international tourist concessions and advice.

Car

There can be no better way to see Australia than by car, camper, or motorcycle. Either renting or buying is straightforward—with some cautions: when purchasing a vehicle it is much safer to buy from a licensed dealer. In Australia a dealer might not be any more or less honest than in your country, but he is governed by consumer protection laws that ensure that there is no "winding back of the clock" (tampering with the odometer), or other malpractice; and that for vehicles over a certain price a warranty must be provided. Becoming a member of a road organization (found through a travel agent or car sales/rental company, or see the list on page 163) entitles you to roadside repairs, towing, and the provision of advice and maps. Be careful of Backpacker companies (see Backpackers, on page 125), which sometimes offer station wagons that have circumnavigated the country more times than you might wish.

All of the above can be explored through your travel agent, or, more conveniently, on the

Internet (try Google Search or Alta Vista, or the like: Travel information Australia).

The Law

If you are a foreign visitor intending to drive, you should carry an International Driver's License, obtainable from your home country before you leave. This will entitle you to rent and drive a car in all states.

Each state has its own driving license, and its own local rules. It is obligatory on your part that you know and observe these rules, particularly the speed limits. Local police may be tolerant with foreign visitors about minor breaches, but not about speeding. You can obtain a copy of local driving rules from the government department in charge of roads and traffic in each state—check the telephone book, or ask a local travel agent or the car-rental company.

Drinking and Driving—Don't Do It!

Random breath testing of drivers for alcohol consumption is carried out in all states. You may be stopped and tested by police at any time.

If the police are called to the scene of an accident, they are also likely to carry out a breath test. However slight the accident may be, if a foreign visitor is involved the other driver might well call the police because of doubts about insurance coverage.

The amount of alcohol you can consume before it becomes illegal to drive varies slightly between states. So do the penalties—if you are caught driving over the limit—from extremely heavy fines to jail terms. A blood alcohol level over .05 percent could well lead to a fine and the loss of your driver's license. Most Australians who intend to drink will nominate a nondrinking driver, or else use a cab.

Taxis

As is the case anywhere in the world, taxis are not cheap. Fares vary from state to state. As the roughest guide to fares: in Sydney in 2014, flag-fall (turning on the meter) is $3.60, then you pay $2.19 per kilometer traveled, plus, if you made a telephone booking, a fee of $2.50. Cab fares from the airports to the city centers are comparable. A lone passenger may choose to sit up front next to the driver. Most drivers are honest, though of course you should make sure that the meter goes on, and it is a good idea to note the driver's number, which is displayed above the windshield, in case you leave something behind when you alight. As a tip, give 10 or 15 percent, or round up the fare to the next dollar.

Taxi-driving is not a long-term profession, so you may well strike someone who is new to the job and not necessarily aware of the shortest route. It's worth checking a map yourself, for an idea of how to get to your destination. If you need to complain for any reason, you should call up the cab company.

DRIVING IN THE OUTBACK

There are some important rules to remember, particularly if you are planning to travel long distances from towns. If you break the rules, the consequences could be very serious. Plan your trip carefully, and get advice about every aspect.

Remember to take off the fan belt when driving through deep water to avoid splashing the engine's

DOS AND DON'TS

- It is essential to have a reliable, good-sized, four-wheel-drive vehicle. Carry spare parts (and know how to fit them), spare gasoline, and water.
- In addition to a GPS / Sat Nav system, have good road maps, and become familiar with them. Find out the state of the roads, particularly if you are going off well-used routes. Tracks through the outback can be very difficult. You should know the distance and timing of each day's journey, and the kind of weather (such as heavy rain or excessive heat) and anything else you are likely to experience.
- Carry food and plenty of drinking water (this is most important).

electrics. You will probably get through water in a creek or river provided that it does not come up much over the bottom of the car door. You must have someone—preferably someone who can swim—walking carefully ahead through creek beds and the like to indicate depths and muddy bottoms. (By the way, crocodiles do not much like running or flooding water.) If you do get stuck in mud or sand, first try letting the air pressure in your tires down so that they are nearly flat; put the car in second or third gear so as not to over rev; and drive using the hand-brake to stop the wheels from spinning. If this fails you will need to raise each rear wheel on the wheel-jack and place underneath them anything you can find to cover the mud or sand. Use cardboard boxes, branches, stones—anything on which your tires can get a grip.

If you are venturing into desert country, advise someone, preferably the police, of your destination and your estimated time of arrival. Arrange to call them to advise of your safe arrival.

If you break down, do not leave the car. Your chances of being seen or found are far better if you stay with your vehicle. Every year in the Australian outback someone leaves his or her car to walk for help and perishes, quite quickly, in the heat.

Hitchhiking
Hitchhiking is illegal in some states, but in any case it is best avoided, especially if you are alone, or even with a companion. Australia has had its share of hitchhiking rapes and murders.

ACCOMMODATION
Backpackers
In Australia the word "hostel" has mostly become "backpackers," or "backpacker

hostel." Along with the name change has come a marked improvement in quality as well as quantity (they are to be found all over Australia). Many offer private rooms with *en-suite* bathrooms as well as small dormitories for groups of two to eight, and bigger ones for up to twenty. Some have bars and restaurants, twenty-four hour opening, tour booking facilities, laundry facilities, communal lounges, and general notice boards.

Backpacker hostels are cheaper than motels, guesthouses, "bed and breakfasts," and most hotels. They can stand alone, or be part of a pub or a caravan park. Wherever you are there will be Internet cafés to enable you to access e-mail accounts such as Hotmail or Yahoo. (You can set up a free account by going to www.hotmail.com or www.yahoo.com, and you will find a list of Australian Internet cafés.)

There are a number of backpacker hostel chains operating throughout Australia, including the YHA, YIP, NOMADS, YMCA, and YWCA.

Not So Cheap
If you want, and are prepared to pay for, something more than a backpacker hostel, there are various options. Throughout Australia there are hotels and motels with good, comfortable accommodation, with standards rising to luxury level. There are stringent government and local council controls, particularly in areas such as

general cleanliness, and the storage, preparation, and supply of food.

All cities, larger towns, and tourist resorts offer first-class accommodation for businesspeople and other travelers. Of course, these are not generally cheap, but having said that, there are certainly some bargains to be had, and these are best sought out on the Internet.

There are "bed-and-breakfast" places throughout the country—but caution: these are not the equivalent of the modest "bed and breakfasts" found in Europe. Most of them offer accommodation of very high quality, complete with designer furnishings and expensive fittings. They are vastly superior to backpackers; in fact they are near the top of the accommodation hierarchy, and many of them also offer gourmet dinners at restaurant prices.

HEALTH AND SECURITY

The sun is often far more dangerous than the creatures mentioned below. You should *never* venture out in the sun without using a sun-block cream or lotion with a UV factor of 15 or higher (clearly marked on the package) applied to every exposed part of your skin—women should apply this routinely under their make-up. Also, you should never stay out in direct sun for more than a few minutes without a hat. Avoid the sun between 11:00 a.m. and 3:00 p.m. If you do get sunburned, you should immediately apply ice wrapped in a cloth (not directly), or get under cool running water. If it is serious, go to a doctor.

The availability of free health care varies depending on your country of origin. As an intending visitor to Australia, especially if you are planning so stay for an extended time, you should check with your embassy, and with an Australian embassy or consulate, to determine your travel insurance coverage. You should do this before you leave your country.

At the front of the telephone directory of each state capital (in the A–K volume for those states with two volumes), you'll find a great variety of health and other care organizations. Emergency services, public hospitals, narcotics anonymous, alcoholics anonymous, sexual assault counseling, suicide prevention, medical specialists, and community help for young people, are among the many services available to anyone in need.

Should you be in need of any help, do not hesitate to go to the nearest police station. You will find them very willing to assist you.

The Bush: Creepies and Crawlies

No kind of creature poses a greater or more constant threat to human well-being than we ourselves do. Compared to the harm that people do to each other, accidentally or maliciously, the impact of other species is seldom momentous. Yet it can be disquieting.

For animals to have power over us is an affront to our notions of environmental mastery, arousing emotions derived from a primitive fear—an inheritance from ancient man's struggle to survive in a world inhabited by many more dangerous creatures than exist today.

As a visitor to Australia you will be at far greater risk of being run over by a tour bus than of being bitten by anything very nasty. Many Australians have never seen a snake in its natural environment; few have encountered a funnel-web spider. With sensible care, you won't, either. These creatures live in their own environment, and it is only if you move into that environment that you will be at any risk at all, and then it will be minimal. Taking the following precautions will ensure your safety.

If you walk in the bush (the outback, rural land), keep to the well-traveled tracks, and you will almost certainly not meet any snakes. They much prefer their own company, and will keep away from the sound of walkers. They are sensitive to vibrations, will know you are coming a long time before you have any chance of seeing them, and will generally move out of the way. Very few attacks, according to the experts, are the result of treading on snakes in grass. Most result from acts of bravado or fear. People try to catch or harass them, when all they have to do is let them slip away. If you must move off well-traveled tracks, it is a good idea to carry a staff (a long stick) and occasionally hit the grass as you walk. But it is better not to tempt fate—have a happy holiday by being sensible and keeping to places where other people walk.

If you follow the above advice, you will not need to know the next bit—but it must be said. If the worst happens, and you are bitten, forget the old instructions about cutting the wound or sucking out the venom. Wrap a bandage firmly over the bite area and then up toward your heart, and get help or get to a doctor immediately.

If you are of a nervous disposition, don't read this paragraph. Many Australian snakes are venomous, and some are extremely potent. At least ten of them are more lethal than an Indian cobra. America's most feared rattlesnake would barely rank in Australia's top twenty.

There are lots of spiders; most of them are harmless, but some are poisonous. They are mostly in the bush, so if you are out walking or camping, be aware of them and where they are. Again, stay out of their area.

Be cautious of overhanging bushes or branches if you can't see clearly through them. Do not put your fingers under pieces of bark or wood, or turn stones over carelessly. Shift them slightly first, and then tilt them toward you so that you can

see underneath, if you have to pick them up. As a
general rule, don't touch spiders with bodies larger
than your little fingernail. Better still, don't touch
any of them. If one gets on your clothes, shake
it off (don't brush it off with your hand). When
picnicking or camping, shake out your blankets,
groundsheets, sleeping bags, and the like. Check
your shoes before you put them on. If one gets on
your skin, take a deep breath and allow it to walk
off—again, do not brush at it with your hand.

Once again, if you are nervous, don't read the
following. The most dangerous (probably the
world's deadliest) spider, the funnel-web spider,
is found in the southern and eastern states. Most
Australians have never seen one. These spiders
like damp, dark undergrowth, away from tracks
and paths, and venture out mostly at night. They
can be deadly.

One spider that is found all around Australia
(and is rarely deadly) is the redback—a small but
nasty little creature that has taken to living in
man-made structures and materials that people
leave around—old tins, rubbish, fence-posts,
and the like. Don't pick it up! There is antivenin
available for both these and other spiders. If you
should be bitten, bandage over the bite and toward
your heart, and seek medical help *immediately*.

Walking
Similar rules apply elsewhere. On land, stick
to established paths and walkways. Wear solid

walking shoes or boots, and thick socks. Be watchful in caves, and when walking under low branches and through dense vegetation. Be careful where you put your hands.

At the beach, it is generally safe to walk barefoot on the sand, but before you do so look and see whether other people are doing the same thing. The swimming beaches you are likely to visit will be quite safe, but make sure that you are not venturing where the locals are not going.

It is not so safe to walk in water over rocks without shoes and without care (never run—the force of a running foot heightens the danger). There are a couple of venomous creatures that can inflict serious wounds. One, the stonefish, is found mostly on coasts of Queensland, the Northern Territory, and northern Western Australia; the other, the blue-ringed octopus, may be found in any rock pools on the coast. Go only where you see the locals go.

The Sea—Monsters of the Deep

Not all these monsters are living. Rips (narrow currents of water racing out to sea), surf, and rocks cause many more deaths than sharks. To avoid these monsters, obey the following rules.

Never swim alone, and swim only on beaches manned by lifeguards, or where the local people are swimming with their children. Do not swim in surf if you are not used to it. You will probably see teenagers with surfboards, but you should note that they are accomplished surf swimmers, and often surf where it is not safe for visitors to swim. You should swim only in the area *between* the flags placed on the beach to show where it is safe, and patrolled, not outside the flags. Do not dive into the water from rocks, reefs, cliffs, or pontoons.

The Queensland and Northern Territory coasts are very dangerous from October to May. Check for jellyfish. A couple of these (the sea wasp and the box jellyfish) have virtually invisible tentacles that are capable of inflicting fatal stings.

Crocodiles are found year-round in northern Australia, inland in rivers and creeks, in estuaries, and on the coasts. Read up on any area you are visiting, and follow the advice of the locals. If there is no advice available, then don't swim.

Keep a sense of humor, follow the rules, and your holiday will be memorable for the right reasons. Happy traveling!

BUSINESS BRIEFING

"THE AUSTRALIAN WAY"

Business attitudes derive in part from the structures of the economy, their history, and the consequences of successive governments' attempts to control elements such as inflation, taxes, employment, and the like.

Before you venture into doing any business in Australia, it might be a good idea to familiarize yourself with some of the background, so that you will understand what has brought about "the Australian way." This will contribute to your business relationships and discussions with Australians, who have strong feelings for their links with the past, whether they and their families stem from early settlers or from more recent immigration.

The Australian economy has historically been seen to have a clear, cyclical, boom-bust patterns, for example in the real estate market, the stock market, and interest rates. This might be lessening as successive Treasurers have searched for steadier development; however, the pattern is unlikely to disappear. To state the obvious but important fact, either you will arrive in a period of boom, with high real estate values and sales, strong stock market, relatively high interest rates, and so on, or you will hit a period of bust, with largely opposite indicators. It may be somewhere in between the two. You need to know! If nothing else—the exchange rate of the Australian dollar with your own country's currency may affect your travel budget and plans.

A POCKET ECONOMIC HISTORY
The original settlers faced an unfamiliar, barren land, and struggled to produce enough food simply to feed themselves and their families. In the late eighteenth and early nineteenth centuries, large-scale sheep farming provided a new way of making a living. Land that would not support the usual crops (mostly wheat, barley, and oats) was used as grazing land. It was said that the Australian economy "rode on the sheep's back." Wool was still the biggest export earner as recently as 1989.

In the period from the 1820s, explorers and other pioneers found land suited to cattle raising, and many settlers started cattle stations (ranches).

The historical links with England provided a
ready market for Australian wool, lamb, beef,
and wheat.

For a long time Australia has been the Lucky
Country. If you didn't grow it or graze it, you
dug it up. Australia has vast mineral supplies and
other natural resources: iron ore, gold, bauxite,
oil, natural gas, zinc, lead, nickel, and copper—
and coal reserves for smelting. Of perhaps more
interest than importance, Australia produces
almost all of the world's opals, and large
quantities of diamonds and sapphires.

More recently, Australia entered the
technological world. In the late 1940s the Snowy
Mountains Hydroelectric Scheme employed

thousands of European immigrants in harnessing the waters of the Snowy River (on the border of New South Wales and Victoria) for the production of electricity and irrigation further downstream. In the same period, Australia built its first motor car, the Holden. Sadly, in a sign of the times, much of Australia's motor manufacturing industry has closed down, as it struggles to compete with manufacturers in China, South Africa, and South America.

Australians are also resourceful on a small scale—they tend to invent things they can make in the back shed. Some of the more interesting of these inventions are described opposite. On a larger scale, many lament the lack of innovation in Australian industry these days—in particular the fact that Australians export basic goods that other countries than manufacture and sell on as a more sophisticated produced—at a much greater profit margin. For example, while

Australia is a premier exporter of wool, the rights to the iconic Aussie "ugg boot" are now owned by an American manufacturer, and the official "ugg" footwear is no longer made in Australia.

Great Australian Firsts

The Stump Jump Plow

In 1870 a bolt broke from farmer Richard Smith's plow. He found that it then moved more easily over stumps and stones, so he went home and perfected the pivoting share that now slides over Australian farmland.

The "Ute"

In 1932, Lewis Brandt, a twenty-two-year-old Australian designer with the Ford Motor Company, drew up plans for a vehicle in which a farmer could take his family to church on Sunday and his pigs to market on Monday. It came to be called a utility truck, or "Ute," but back in Detroit Henry Ford called it a "kangaroo chaser."

Aspro

Pharmacist George Nicholas, in Melbourne, developed this pain reliever based on aspirin in 1917; by 1940 it had become the world's most widely used headache treatment.

Ultrasound

Developed in 1961 by scientists from the Commonwealth Health Department, this method of testing the health of unborn babies without X-rays is used around the world.

The Bionic Ear
In 1978 a team led by Professor Graeme Clark implanted a bundle of fine electrodes into the ear of a man who had become totally deaf in a car accident. After some months of fine tuning, he could hear again. A company called Cochlear Pty Ltd sells the technology to the world.

The Wine Cask
A plastic bag filled with wine inside a cardboard box was developed by Thomas Angove, the head of a South Australian wine company. These are now used worldwide, though are less popular in Australia than they used to be.

The "Esky"
A company called Malleys saw the need in 1950 for a portable beer cooler. They made a steel box in a steel box that could be filled with iced water, and named it the "Eskimos." In the 1970s the esky became plastic—and could hold more beer.

Australia today is much less dependent on the export of primary products. In fact a very big market for the export of food to the UK was lost with their entry into the European Community. Other industries have taken its place. Tourism is a large and growing industry, and Australian universities cater to thousands of students from Southeast Asia. Service industries have grown to cope with local business requirements.

The changes in economic emphasis, some recent and radical, to increased industrialization, have led to more openness in business attitudes. You will find Australian businessmen and women open to new ideas and recent developments. If you can demonstrate that you are informed and knowledgeable—without having to resort to your briefing book or Powerpoint slides—you'll gain credibility. Australians are busy, dynamic, and pragmatic; they will not appreciate their time being wasted.

Organization charts tend to be flatter—less hierarchical—than is the case in some countries, such as France, Germany, and Japan. Senior decision makers are generally more accessible, particularly, but not only, in smaller companies. So, when seeking to present yourself, or your products, or services, go to the top. Find out who is the most senior person in your area and try to speak with him or her directly to make an appointment. If this is not possible, send an e-mail directly to that person.

WOMEN ON TOP?

Little needs to be said, apart from the fact that women are there, perhaps underrepresented in terms of numbers, but very much making their mark in leadership positions Chances are, therefore, that if you become involved in business in Australia, that you will find yourself conducting your business with as many women as men. There's nothing much more that needs to be said, as there are no special rules of protocol or etiquette in terms of dealing with women in management. Whether attributable to the increasing presence of women, the Australia workplace is, these days, a bit more "PC" (politically correct) and the "blokey" culture and old boys' network that dominated certain banks and law firms have gone the way of the liquid (alcohol sodden) lunch.

THE WORK ETHIC

For some reason—perhaps partly because of their fondness for sport and for spending their weekends with their families—Australian workers have carried the stigma of being less than hardworking. It is also possible that this stemmed from the early power of the trade unions, for over the last fifty years or more they strived for better work conditions, more appropriate working hours, and better pay rates, sometimes with militancy and calls for "All out!"

Twenty or more years ago the phrase, "She'll be right" alluded not only to Australians' attitude to social life, but perhaps to work and business as well. Certainly union strikes and demarcation disputes (which worker from which union could do which job) were notorious, a way of life. And certainly workers won the right to advantages like the extraordinary "leave loading" (under which rules workers are paid more—a loading—when they are on holiday than when they are working). No more. Australians are "up there" with other OECD countries in hours worked and, in a recent survey of sick days taken, "up there" in the lowest number of lost days. You can expect your business contacts to be hardworking—and they will expect you to be the same.

Australian workers, through their trade unions, won their basic rights over a long period of disputes and strikes. The eight-hour day was secured by striking stonemasons in 1855, the basic minimum wage in 1907, and the forty-hour week in 1946. The world's first legislation providing for paid sick leave and paid "long-service" leave was enacted in the state of New South Wales in 1951. You will find some Australians to be at once proud of the achievements of workers through their trade unions and, to a degree, disdainful of some of the union tactics. You will find a few workers who are very antimanagement, and some few managers who are scornful of the unions. You will also hear long debates between the two major political parties and alternating policies (depending which party's in Government) regarding the status of industrial relations legislation, unfair dismissal minimum wage, etc. In fact, under the eleven years of the (Conservative) Liberal/National party coalition Government, their "work choices" policy attempted to individualize employment relations and, as a consequence, to marginalize both trade unions and industrial tribunals. But mostly you will find that workers are proud of their trades, and good at them, and that most managers respect the unions and are happy to be working with them.

While it is true that many Australians work to live (thinking that people from some countries seem to live to work), they work hard to achieve the lifestyle they have.

MAKING APPOINTMENTS

Personal relationships are important in doing business in Australia, especially for visiting businesspeople. The people you are wishing to meet will understand this, so if you have made a contact who could be helpful in getting you an appointment, ask him or her for help. However, you should be aware that although "helping" may extend this far, and may get you a friendly welcome, it does not extend to supporting your business or your proposition. Once in the interview or meeting, you are on your own.

Keep detailed notes on everyone you meet or hear referred to, and on their business and their roles. You may ask someone with whom you have gained an appointment if they can recommend someone else you should see, either in their own organization or in others. Linkedin, the professional social website, has proven to be a useful tool for keeping your network—and your own profile and CV—current.

Appointments should be made ahead by telephone. Ask for the person whom you wish to meet. You might be lucky, particularly in a smaller company, and be put straight through to speak to him or her, which would obviously be better than having to explain your position through a third party. However, it is quite likely that you will find yourself speaking to a personal assistant or secretary. Be ready to explain your position. Make it clear that you are a foreign visitor, and do not be afraid to ask for assistance. Most Australians will respond to a plea for help.

MEETINGS AND NEGOTIATION

There will be differences between big and small businesses, and these cannot really be established until you visit (unless you have information from someone else). Many companies do business with overseas companies, and personnel in these companies are used to dealing with people from a range of cultures. They are likely to adapt quite readily to different kinds of humor, modes of address, and levels of formality.

It is standard business practice for men to wear a suit and for women to be similarly professionally attired, but be prepared to take your jacket off if your host does so. Everyone shakes hands in business situations, and, unless dealing with very senior management or politicians, quickly moves to first-name terms.

Many people, particularly in creative circles, such as IT, publishing, advertising, and so on, now dress and operate in a much more informal way, with many working partly from home, and only donning a suit for business meetings.

Offer your business card at the start of the meeting, and be prepared to answer questions such as, "How long have you been in Australia— and how do you like it so far?" However, casual and friendly as they might appear, Australian businessmen and women will want to get down to business, and will appreciate a readiness to do so. Outline your purpose in calling the meeting, and make your proposals with openness, directness, and brevity.

Australians accept negotiation as part of a business proposition. Be aware that, generally, you are negotiating from a position of weakness, in that you are on your host's home turf and playing by his or her rules. Listen and learn as quickly as possible just what the rules are—they will vary from company to company, and from individual to individual. Australians will be more impressed by your questions than by your statements. Be sure that you have gathered all available information before you begin to make your proposal. Be aware of your host's body language; if you do go too far in negotiation you will see a shift in attitude, such as tenseness in body, or terseness in language.

A sense of humor is invaluable. Many an exploratory question, suggestion, or offer can be made with humor and will be accepted in kind. Australians really appreciate people who can "give as good as they get" and be prepared to laugh at themselves, at their profession or occupation, or at their country. Be businesslike but relaxed.

MAKING A PRESENTATION

Keep your presentation factual, with details, specifications, and well-researched documentation. Australians often do not respond well to American-style "bells and whistles" presentations—many of them work for American subsidiaries and have learned to suppress the cynicism and eye-rolling.

Because you are a foreign visitor, and especially if what you are presenting is new to them, you can expect Australians to be concerned with historical data, testimonials, and references. Expect searching questions on business models used and data presented.

After or during your presentation you are likely to be questioned, and you will be expected to have done your homework in any areas that affect your proposal, such as customs, imports, money transfers, government regulations and approvals, and foreign investment; and also any relevant local issues, such as workplace agreements, industrial relations, and so on. It would be sensible to contact the Australian Trade Commission at the Australian Embassy or Consulate in your country before you leave home, to get the appropriate information and advice on such matters before preparing your presentation. You might also find useful information on the Internet. The following Web sites might be helpful:

www.austrade.gov.au (Australian Trade Commission)

www.customs.gov.au (Import Trade Assistance)

www.dewr.com.au (Department of Employment and Workplace Relations)

www.oer.com.au (Australian Workplace Agreement)

EGALITARIANISM IN THE WORKPLACE

Australians do believe in equality—to a degree. This does not mean that they think workers on the factory floor should earn as much as senior managers, or that they should receive the same benefits. However, this is not because workers themselves, as individuals, are considered to be in any way less worthy, but just that the position they hold in the company does not make the same demands on them (in education, experience, qualification, and personal responsibility).

What are respected are individual ethics, work habits, general knowledge, and talents, along with success in relationships, and strong family values—and the certain knowledge that senior managers in no way alone have these virtues. Thus, the proverb "Jack is as good as his master" may sound like anachronistic language —but the attitude still holds true.

Friendships are often made across hierarchies—managers will have a drink, play football or go running or to the gym together at lunchtime with staff of different levels, even though such matters as income, politics, and lifestyle may separate them socially.

BUSINESS AND SOCIALIZING

Australians will tell you that the days of the
"free lunch" are over. This alludes to the days
when company entertainment of clients was tax-
deductible as legitimate investment expenditure;
many of the older managers remember them
with nostalgia. Friday lunch was routine and
often morphed into after-work drinks. Afternoon
drinks sealed many a deal, and golf was affordable.
Not any more. You are over twenty years too late.

Any drinking to which you are invited today
will be less of a "free for all". Some company
personnel, particularly in a small company, might
invite you to lunch, or to a drink after work—
but don't be disappointed if they don't. Such an
invitation is the exception rather than the rule.

If you are invited to lunch, your hosts will be
unlikely to drink much alcohol—if at all (unless
the occasion is a special occasion, such as a deal
closing), and you would be wise to follow suit.
But if they do drink, and if your meeting has not
been completed, a decision on your part to refuse
alcohol will certainly be respected. On that note, if
you don't drink alcohol, don't use this as a reason
to refuse an invitation to a drink after work, or
after the successful completion of an agreement.
It will be accepted if you explain that you do not
drink alcohol, and ask for something soft.

If you do find yourself at a club or pub with
business associates, do not forget your "shout"—
your turn to buy the drinks.

chapter nine

COMMUNICATING

AUSTRALIAN ENGLISH—SPEAKING "STRINE"

They speak English, don't they? Well, yes . . . but it is often a very special brand of English. The earliest Australian immigrants were a mixture of Irish and English convicts, soldiers (comprising a lot of Cockneys and other Londoners, a few North Countrymen, and some Scots), and a number of educated naval officers. Then better-educated free settlers began to arrive, particularly in South Australia and Western Australia. This mixture of tongues has mutated into a general Australian English, or "Strine" ("Australian," said in Australian English), with some regional and elective differences. Rather than adding to or altering the language very much, later immigrants from Europe, and even later ones from Asia, have generally adopted Strine, but in keeping their own accents have often produced amazing results.

Be warned—it's very catching. Immigrants with children are often quite horrified, to begin with, when their children become fluent Strine speakers within months of meeting their new mates at school and playing with them "on Sat'di arvo" (on Saturday afternoon).

In an endeavor to capture the tone, actors from overseas are advised to raise the pitch a bit (speaking at a slightly higher level), breathe the words out through the nose, and end sentences with the upward lilt English normally reserves for questions. Try it, for fun—but caution: Strine is very individual. The accent is the butt of much humor, as in: Patient to doctor: "Did I come here to die?" Doctor: "No, mate, you came yesterdie."

The art of brevity, reducing any word to its diminutive, is an essential part of speaking Strine. Postman is usually "postie," car registration is "rego," journalist is "journo," musician is "muso." Even a U-turn (when driving a car) is a "u-ie." And we "chuck a u-ie" when we make a U-turn (chuck being to throw). "G'day mate," tends to be used by older Australians, and "youse" as in—"how youse goin?" is the language of the wharfies—not the yachties.

Names are also subject to diminution. Any man with red hair is, of course, called Blue. Prince Philip is Phil the Greek and all Warrens are called Rabbit. Poor old Mark Waugh, a cricketer whose uneven performance had him constantly compared unfavourably with his more successful cricketing brother, Steve, earned the nickname "Korea" —as in "the forgotten Waugh" (war). You will find a glossary of Strine and some diminutives on page 162.

TELEPHONE AND INTERNET

Emergencies
Police, Ambulance, Fire 000
From a cell phone 000 or 112
Services
Directory assistance national 1223
Directory assistance international 1225

Directories

Even in the Internet age, Australia still insists on destroying trees to deliver each household a "Yellow Pages" phone directory.

Each city has a Telstra White Pages telephone directory. In the larger cities, this runs to two volumes: A–K and L–Z. Regardless of the number of volumes, the layout is roughly the same in all of them.

At the front of the directory (or at the front of the A–K volume) you will find:

- Listings for federal, state, and local government services (traffic, health, education, aged care)
- Emergency information
- Telephone information (phone cards, directory information, call costs, overseas calls)
- Public transport information

In the main section of each directory (spread across two volumes) you will find:

- Business listings in alphabetical order
- Residential listings in alphabetical order

At the back of each directory (or at the back of the L–Z volume) you will find:

- Place-names and abbreviations
- International telephone codes

The "Yellow Pages" is a directory of businesses, products, and services, containing emergency numbers, community services, essential services, help lines, rescue services, specialized health organizations, etc.

Australia's residential telephone directories are available on the Internet (www.whitepages.com.au and www.yellowpages.com.au).

Service Providers

The main communications carriers in Australia are Telstra, Optus, and Vodaphone, all of which offer "bundled" services for combining a number of family members' cell phones, landlines, and, in the case of Telstra, cable TV. All will also offer special global roaming deals, and "pay as you go" plans; phone cards, naturally, can be readily purchased from these carriers or convenience stores or newsagents.

Australians and visitors alike have long been frustrated by slow speed of, and patchy access to, the country's broadband Internet services. In 2009 the government announced the roll out of the NBN—the National Broadband Network—a government business enterprise designed to deliver and operate Australia's first national open access broadband network, and create a competitive market for retail broadband and telephone services. Telstra was formerly the government domestic telecommunication service until its phased privatization was completed in 2006.

Since deregulation of the Australian telecommunications industry in the 1990s, Telstra has managed to stay way ahead of rivals Optus and Vodaphone and remain the largest telecommunications provider. This success is partly due to its low rates on some routes and at certain times, its ability to "bundle" phone services together with cable TV, and its recent re-branding which included a strong customer service focus. In 2014, Telstra was named "most respected company" by the *Australian Financial Review* newspaper. If you are planning on spending some time in Australia, use your search engine to find one of the websites that will compare prices and services of the different telecomm carriers for you.

Call Cards

In Australia prepaid phone cards or calling cards are a cheap way of calling overseas, interstate or mobiles. There are an increasing number of Australian pre-paid phonecards with different call rates to different countries. Again, there are numerous Web sites showing comparative prices to different countries. Phone cards can be purchased from the major telecommunications company retail stores (easily found in shopping malls or airports)—or from newsagents, convenience stores, or the post office.

POST

Post offices (with the insignia "P" in a circle, white on red) are open between 9:00 a.m. and 5:00 p.m. throughout cities, suburbs, and country towns, in all states. Some open on Saturday mornings.

Next-day postal services apply intrastate, and usually two-day services interstate (this may differ in country towns). There is usually one postal delivery per day in cities and metropolitan areas; the service is less frequent in some country towns and homes in the outback.

Post offices are retail outlets selling stamps, envelopes and boxes for both normal, certified, express delivery services, greeting cards, toys, and other stationery Local residents can pay some

utility charges and other bills there, too. For more information dial 13 13 17, or go to www.auspost.com.au.

COMMUNICATION STYLES

Australians generally (and it *is* a generalization) dislike pretentiousness, and are unpretentious themselves. The best way to "prove yourself" as a visitor to Australia is by being authentic, and not trying too hard. If you "talk yourself up" (brag or boast) you'll be said to "have tickets on yourself" be conceited or arrogant.

As you have read, people from all over the world have immigrated to Australia, have been tested out and teased by Aussies to see if the "blow in" (newcomer) can give as good as they get.

If you engage in this verbal sparring, show that you're quick witted, and demonstrate a sense of humor—then you'll win the Aussies round.

Most Australians will prefer to get to know you gradually. They would probably like to hear about your background, education, areas of expertise, special skills, and the like—but over a period of time. They will decide whether they like you on the basis of who you are—not on your achievements or lengthy CV. It is a lesson that some overseas visitors, who often seem to aggravate Australians, would do well to learn.

You don't have to prove anything—unless, of course, you fail to return the hospitality of your new-found Australian mates and fail to "shout" a round of drinks, in which case you will quickly become a "bloody bludger" (a "bludger" being someone who doesn't pull their weight or pay their share). On that note, it is worth remarking that some of what the rest of the world considers to be bad language or swearing has a different connotation and use in Australia. If you come from a background where profanity is, well, for the profane, or the uncouth, you may well be in for a shock.

The prime example is that great Australian adjective, "bloody." This causes great offense to some Americans, but it must be said that it does not carry any particular meaning in Australia. "Bloody" is simply a bit more colorful than its predecessor, "damned." What used to be "Close the damned door, will you?" has become, "Close the bloody door, will you?" It is simply an expletive, used for emphasis. It may suggest a lack of ability to use appropriate adjectives, but it is not meant to be offensive.

Even more paradoxical is the use (primarily among males) of the word "bastard." You need to know that in Australia this is rarely an insult, being used warmly and humorously in such phrases as, "G'day, you old bastard!" and "How you goin', you old bastard?" These are, simply, affectionate greetings. Women are rarely addressed in this way, Australian men readily use this kind of language with each other, but will often tone it down in the presence of women. However, women, too, will often have a bloody good swear, if the situation warrants! The f*** word (which is increasingly used by the younger generation) is still fundamentally taboo, as are some other unpleasant words.

Serious or Humorous?

Australians appreciate humor, both in business and socially. Humor is used particularly as a "defence mechanism", to defuse tension, or, with liberal use of sarcasm and irony, to convey a home truth. Given the choice, choose humor every time. Well, *nearly* every time. There is nothing funny about Australia losing a Test Match, or against the Kiwis (New Zealand) at Rugby; and there's nothing funny about losing that business deal to a Pommy rival, or a good bottle of Shiraz getting tipped over.

Really, there is very little that Australians do not make fun of. Their humor will often be sacrilegious; the freedom to satirize anyone is fundamental to democracy. Jokes made at the expense of certain minority groups, or those who are, or would be, unable to defend themselves, however, are considered offensive. Those in positions of power are fair game, and favorite targets are politicians, bosses, the police—and visitors. You should know that it is mandatory to be able to take a joke. For example, few Australians would ever wear socks with sandals, and the European males who do so are always good for a laugh. On a more serious note, when it comes to attire, Australians generally won't give a second glance to an Indian taxi driver wearing a turban, or the female IT manager who wears a hijab scarf to cover her head and neck. There is a time in business dealings to forgo the humor. For you, that is. Your host will retain the right to have a joke at your expense, in which case you can join in with a quick retort—but make it a good one.

Most Australians reckon that it's a rough day if you can't have a laugh.

CONCLUSION

So you are going to Australia, and, yes, it's a bloody long plane ride. But your visit can offer such rich rewards that it shouldn't be missed. As you have seen, a traveler will find very little sameness. Diversity is the hallmark of Australia and of Australian life.

Australia's ties to other countries—and consequent sense of identity—can be described as a "mixed bag." Australia is still a member of the British Commonwealth. Many Australians are monarchists, and constitutional and emotional links with the "mother country" are strong. However, immigration and the changing demographic face of twenty-first century Australia has brought with it close ties to many other European and Asian countries.

Not so fixed are the economic links. Since the formation of the European Economic Community, Australia has lost much of its European export market and has turned to Southeast Asia. However, the USA is the biggest foreign investor in Australia, followed by the UK, Singapore, and Japan, and the USA and UK are also the top destinations for Australian investments abroad (nearly 45 percent). So the key to Australia's psyche is, again, diversity—of cultural, emotional, and economic links.

In this book you have read of certain Australian characteristics. The Australians do work to live—but remember, if you should join the workforce, they work hard at their jobs too. They allow full rein to their sense of humor, and it will often be at your expense—but generally only if they like you. They tend to be egalitarian—as a visitor to their home you will be made extremely welcome—as long as you do not tell them for a while that you are very wealthy, very educated, very talented, or very important (in which case you'll be told, in no uncertain terms, to "pull your head in").

But, beyond all that, Australians are very *human,* in the sense that, like all of us, they are proud of their country. They want you to enjoy it, and they like hearing appreciation expressed by visitors. If you like something, tell them.

Australians tend also to be honest and unpretentious. After you get to know them it will be understood that you may find some things difficult to enjoy (like, for example, the nationally loved yeast extract spread Vegemite). Use some humor, and you will be able to express this too.

Because Australia and Australians are generally welcoming and visitor-friendly, wherever you go, you should try to see and enjoy as much as you can in whatever time you have. Even before you start out, well before you arrive, you are a welcome visitor.

As Australians would say "Go for it!" Show humor, appreciation, and interest —and it will be reciprocated "in spades" by your Aussie hosts. Making friends is inevitable.

Glossary: Strine, and Some Diminutives

Akubra
Classic, broad-brimmed Aussie hat

Arvo
Afternoon, as in "see you Sat'di arvo"

Barbie, bar-b-que
Barbecue. Out-of-doors cooking, mostly meat

Bathers
also swimmers, togs, cossie. Swimming costume

Battler
Worker. Aussie concept of struggler, underdog

Beaut
Great, wonderful

Bludger
Usually "dole-bludger," one living off unemployment benefits

Bottle shop
Wine/beer shop, liquor store

Bowser
Petrol Pump

Brickie
Bricklayer

Chook
Chicken, as in "chook raffle" (raffling a chicken)

Chrissie
Christmas

Cobber
Old word for a mate, little used today

Cocky
Farmer or shepherd

Compo
Compensation, as in worker's compensation

Crook
Ill, sick

Deli
Delicatessen

Dinkum
Honest, true, as in "fair dinkum"

Dob in
Inform on someone, betray

Dough
Money (bread is also money)

Driza-bone
Full-length oilskin overcoat, formerly only used by farmers

Dunny
Outdoors toilet, WC

Esky
Portable cooler for food and drink

Footie
Football—the ball and the game

Globe
Light bulb

Gong
Medal

Grog
Liquor, booze

Jackaroo, Jackeroo
(female, Jillaroo). Working rider on a farm

Jarmies
Pajamas

Larrikin
(usually kindly) Scallywag, mischievous

Ocker
The ultimate uncultured Australian, with beer belly and thongs (sandals)

Pokey
Poker machine, slot machine

Prezzie
A present

Ratbag
Stupid person

Sandgroper
Western Australian, because of the deserts

Sheila
Woman (old slang term)

Shout
Buy a round of drinks

Sickie
A day taken off from work because of sickness

Smoko
Smoke, as in taking a smoking break at work

Spit the dummy
Lose your temper

Strides
Trousers

Stubby
Small bottle of beer, or men's shorts

Swag
Bag or bundle carried by a "swagman," or bush traveler, as in the song "Waltzing Matilda"

Tassie
Tasmania

Tinnie, Tube
Can of beer

Uni
University

Whinger
Complainer, especially as in "Pommy whinger"

Wowser
Puritan, killjoy

Resources

Emergency Number (police, fire, ambulance) 000;

Second Emergency Number from a mobile device 112

Health and Safety

Poisons Information Centre 13 1126

Police for nonemergency situtations in NSW 13 1444

In the online telephone directory for each state are lists of health and other care organizations. These include Public Hospitals, Narcotics Anonymous, Alcoholics Anonymous, Sexual Assault Counseling, Suicide Prevention, Medical Specialists, and Community Help for Young People.

Air Travel

Webjet.com.au for Australian domestic airline fares and schedule comparisons

Qantas 13 1313; www.qantas.com.au

Virgin 13 6789; www.virginaustralia.com

Flight Centre: 133 133 www.flightcentre.com.au This is an Australia-wide travel operator that offers package holidays in Australia and overseas.

Coach Travel

Greyhound 3 2030; www.greyhound.com.au

Australia Wide: Head office Tel. 02 9516 1300 www.austwide.com.au

For local public transport (ferry, rail and bus) use your search engine to find the website for the Australian city or state of interest.

For Sydney, NSW www.transportnsw.info

Car Rental

Avis 13 63333; www.avis.com

Budget 1300 362 848; www.budget.com.au

Hertz 13 3039; www.hertz.com

Thrifty 1300 367 227; www.thrifty.com.au

Accommodation

In addition to YHA Australia (yha.com.au) there are many Web sites for visitors seeking accommodation for backpackers in Australia, in addition to the airbnb option.

Standards of accommodation vary widely so check out review before booking!

For travelers with disabilities information can be found at http://www.disabled-world.com/travel/australia/

Lost or Stolen Credit Cards

Card organizations

Visa (local cardholders) 1800 450 346

Visa (international cardholders) 1800 805 346

American Express 1300 132 639

Further Useful Web Sites

Australian Broadcasting Corporation: www.abc.net.au

Special Broadcasting Services (for multi-cultural Radio & TV): www.sbs.com.au.

Australian Government Funded Job Search Site: www.jobsearch.com.au

Australian Job Search Site: www.seek.com.au

Australian Trade Commission: www.austrade.gov.au

Australia's Internet and Phone Directory: www.citysearch.com.au

Australian Workplace Agreements: www.workplaceinfo.com.au

Department of Immigration: www.immi.gov.au

Information about visiting, working, or studying in Australia http://www.australia.gov.au/topics/immigration

Reciprocal health insurance cover: www.hic.gov.au—Travelers to Australia

Special Broadcasting Services (for multi-cultural Radio & TV): www.sbs.com.au.

Telstra: www.telstra.com

White pages: www.whitepages.com.au

Yellow pages: www.yellowpages.com.au

Internet cafés and general wifi access is plentiful around Australia.

Further Reading

History and Contemporary Affairs

Blainey, Geoffrey. *The Tyranny of Distance*.
Australia: Sun Books, 1975.
Australia's history shaped by its geography and size.

Blainey, Geoffrey. *A Shorter History of Australia*.
Melbourne: Heinemann, 1994.

Chatwin, Bruce. *The Songlines*.
London: Jonathan Cape, 1988.
Insight into Aboriginal beliefs.

Clark, Manning. *A Short History of Australia*.
New York: Penguin, 1981.
The picture up to the 1980s (the full version is in six volumes).

Daly, Margo, et al. *The Rough Guide to Australia*.
London: Rough Guides, 2001.

Harding, Paul, et al. *Lonely Planet: Australia*.
Melbourne/Oakland/London/Paris: Lonely Planet Publications, 2002.

Horne, Donald. *The Lucky Country: Australia in the Sixties*.
Ringwood, Victoria, Australia: Penguin, 1964.
The definitive study reference to Australia.

Morgan, Sally. *My Place*.
New York: Henry Holt, 1988.
London: Virago, 1988.
Biography.

James, Clive. *Unreliable Memoirs: Autobiography*.
London: Picador, 2008.
Humorous autobiography of growing up in Australia in the 1950s.

Pilger, John. *A Secret Country*.
London: Jonathan Cape, 1992.
Pilger is Australia's (and other parts of the world's) conscience.
He shows the other side of contemporary Australia.

further reading

Pusey, Michael. *The Experience of Middle Australia.*
Cambridge: Cambridge University Press, 2003.
The effects of economic globalization and economic rationalism on middle Australia.

Dale, David. *Who We Are: A Miscellany of The New Australia.*
Sydney: Crows Nest, NSW: Allen & Unwin, 2006.
Information and statistics, often in list form, of what it means to be an Australian.

Reynolds, Henry. *The Other Side of the Frontier.*
Townsville: James Cook University, 1981.
Ringwood, Victoria, Australia: Penguin, 1982.
White settlement of Australia—the Aborigine's view.

Summers, Ann. *Damned Whores and God's Police.*
Ringwood, Victoria, Australia: Penguin, 2001.
Describes the attitude of the authorities to female convicts and free settlers and explores the influence of this on the colonies and on modern Australia.

Fiction

Carey, Peter. *True History of the Kelly Gang.*
Hardy, Frank. *Power Without Glory.*
Flanagan, Richard. *Sound of One Hand Clapping*
Franklin, Miles. *My Brilliant Career.*
Jolley, Elizabeth. *My Father's Moon.*
Keneally, Thomas. *The Chant of Jimmie Blacksmith.*
Lindsay, Joan. *Picnic at Hanging Rock.*
Malouf, David. *Johnno*, and other works.
Marshall, Alan. *I Can Jump Puddles.*
Winton, Tim. *Cloudstreet.*

Index

Acknowledgment

I would like to thank BK for her untiring and incisive critiques of the manuscript for this book, and her valuable advice for its improvement.